Spirit of the Wind

Spirit of the Wind

The Story of George Attla,
Alaska's Legendary Sled Dog Sprint Champ

Lew Freedman

Epicenter Press
Alaska Book Adventures

Epicenter Press is a regional press founded in Alaska whose interests include but are not limited to the arts, history, environment, and diverse cultures and lifestyles of the North Pacific and high latitudes. We seek both the traditional and innovative in publishing high-quality nonfiction tradebooks, contemporary art and photography giftbooks, and destination travel guides emphasizing Alaska, Washington, Oregon, and California.

Publisher: Kent Sturgis
Cover Design: Sue Mattson
Inside Design: Sue Mattson
Proofreader: Sherrill Carlson
Printer: Transcontinental Printing

SPIRIT OF THE WIND is a new edition of a book originally published by Stackpole Books as George Attla: Legend of the Sled Dog Trail.

Text © 2000 Lew Freeedman
Cover photos © 2000 Mike Mathers
Library of Congress Catalog Card Number: 00 136168

To order SPIRIT OF THE WIND mail $14.95 plus $4.95 for shipping (Washington residents add $1.30 sales tax) to Epicenter Press, Box 82368, Kenmore, WA 98028; visit our website, EpicenterPress.com; or call 800-950-6663.

Booksellers: Retail discounts are available from our trade distributor, Graphic Arts Center Publishing™, Box 10306, Portland, OR 97210.

First printing February 2001
10 9 8 7 6 5 4 3 2 1
PRINTED IN CANADA

I dedicate this book to my sister Minnie, brother Frank, grandson Stephan, and daughter Barbara, and offer special thanks to Gary, Phyllis, Marilyn, Punky, George III, Dobe, Frankie, Shaylin and Tamara.

——George Attla

Contents

Introduction

I first met George Attla—naturally enough—at the dog races. Not in downtown Anchorage at the Fur Rendezvous World Championship, but at nearby Tudor Track, where most of the early-season sprint races take place.

Mushers often reach the track hours before their race is scheduled to begin. They make sure their dogs are ready to go, but then they often retreat to the warmth of their dog trucks to prepare themselves.

Attla's truck was always easy to spot. As befitted his station in the sport, he had one of the sharpest vehicles. There was no mistaking Attla's rig. A sturdy diesel, it was decorated with red, white and blue Tesoro sponsor logos. On the coldest of days, Attla stayed inside the cab, with the engine and heater running. He chainsmoked as part of his countdown to his race, but also welcomed company.

Late in his career, when Attla was in his fifties, he joked often about his old bones and how it was hard for him to stay warm. But other mushers thought he was sandbagging. Attla has lived in some of the harshest climates in Alaska and everyone knew he was a pretty rugged guy.

It was just part of the psyche game, lulling opponents into

thinking he was over the hill and too old to beat them. It was never clear whether Attla was really fooling anyone, but he must have figured some newcomer would fall for his routine.

One of the things George and I have in common is an interest in the sport of boxing. I used to be a boxing writer. Attla loves the fight game and admires the toughness of the best fighters. One of his favorites is Roberto Duran of Panama. Considered by many to be the greatest lightweight of all time, Duran won championships in four weight classes in a career spanning more than twenty years.

Although Attla is an Athabascan by heritage and Duran's first language is Spanish, I can see how the two tough hombres would have things to chat about if they ever got together.

George is also a big fan of another George. As a man whose own career was notable for its longevity and successes decades apart, it is natural for Attla to be fascinated by George Foreman. Attla won his first world championship sprint title in 1958. He won his tenth in 1982. Foreman won the heavyweight title in the 1970s—and won it again in the 1990s.

In my career as a sportswriter, I have written about thousands of athletes participating in so many sports I've lost count. Few have been as dominant in their games as George Attla. None have overcome as much adversity to achieve so much. And none have had his longevity near the top of a sport. I was just turning seven years old when Attla won his first world championship. I was forty-eight when he entered his last sprint mushing race in his home village of Huslia in 1999.

My first impression of George Attla at the races was of a friendly, candid competitor. He told you what he thought about the day's events and he didn't run off and hide if he had a bad day, as so many professional athletes do nowadays. He didn't duck anybody on the course and he didn't duck the tough questions afterwards. When something went wrong he stood his ground explaining what went wrong. He was pleased when he was successful, but he didn't gloat.

I have always admired excellence in sports. I have always admired individuals who overcame problems to win. And as a sportswriter, I've always admired individuals who were not merely fairweather friends, talking only when they were victorious. There were many things I found to admire in George Attla.

George Attla has led an extraordinary life—an uplifting movie titled "Spirit of the Wind" illustrated the remarkable nature of his rise from a tiny village in Interior Alaska to become the toast of fans. His achievements may never be rivaled by an Alaskan athlete.

The records Attla established in his sport remain untouchable. The triumphs, coupled with the drama and challenges of his life, make for a riveting story.

—Lew Freedman

Chapter 1

Newcomer

The stranger walked with a stiff leg. That was the first thing that you noticed about him. He was tall, close to six feet, with wavy black hair. And when he stood on the back of his sled, ready to push off in the first heat of the 1958 Fur Rendezvous World Championship Sled Dog Race on Anchorage's Fourth Avenue, he had a distinctive bearing.

The fans filling the sidewalks, standing on the packed-down snow, craned for a view as the voice on the loudspeaker echoed in the crisp February afternoon air. Each racer was introduced, name given, hometown listed.

There were big cheers for the familiar names, for the defending champion Gareth Wright of Fairbanks, for the other racers whose biographies were known.

But no one knew the handsome young man from Huslia. His face went unrecognized, and his name meant nothing to the citizens of Alaska's largest city.

"George Attla," said the announcer. Polite applause. Unknowns came and went in the Fur Rendezvous. Sometimes a competitor would show up, race his three heats, and discover that he was not yet ready for such big-time racing, that the dogs that looked so strong and powerful back home in the village were not dogs fit enough for three days of hard racing. And that was the last you'd hear of him. He was a musher going against the world's best one year, a footnote in Rendezvous history the next.

Which would it be for George Attla, this newcomer? Would he become someone special, or would he be one of the many passing through? Three heats of tough running, of twenty-five miles of racing per day, challenged and wore out the best huskies. The Fur Rendezvous, the annual winter carnival that attracted thousands of fans to Anchorage from all over the state, was the showcase race of sprint dog mushing, indeed the showcase competition of the carnival itself. And it was a showcase for the very best dogs with the strongest of hearts and lungs and the sturdiest of legs.

The Rendezvous had its roots in the old trapping lifestyle, with the grizzled men who worked the rugged winter landscape with traplines set out to catch lynx, beaver, and other furbearers. They lived a solitary life in the Bush. Using sleds hauled by dogs through the woods and across the frozen rivers and lakes, they tended their traps. For months they withstood the rigors of vicious weather, high winds, deep snow, and frigid temperatures to earn meager livings. They hunkered down in tiny log cabins in the wilderness, heated only by the fires they built, fueled only by the wood they could gather. It was a throwback lifestyle, the way of life of earlier peoples, not the modern American who has electric conveniences in his home and gets around town in an automobile. No cars, no appliances: you made what you could from the !and, and you lived with it and lived by it.

It was a life for a certain type. Loneliness, though, was a major problem. A man could go crazy sitting there alone in the Alaska winter wild for months. They called it cabin fever, and Rendezvous was the remedy.

In the old days, in gold rush times and after, the trapper looked forward to spring and a celebration. The Fur Rendezvous was a chance not only to sell the fur pelts trapped during the long winter season, but also to kick back and party. That was what Rendezvous was all about. A man had to let loose, didn't he? A man needed to play.

Anchorage formalized this partying in 1946, and it has been a highlight of the winter calendar ever since. Activities span two weeks: there are parties, bake-offs, sporting contests, and competitions to see who has the furriest face or longest beard, and who can drink a glass of beer the quickest. This gives new meaning to the Big Gulp.

But the partying pauses for the dog races. Racing has always been part of the Rendezvous. A musher named Jake Butler won the first world championship, though there were only three finishers. The event gradually grew in popularity with both mushers and fans. The fields grew to twenty or more competitors who raced big teams of twenty well-trained dogs. The fans turned race days into a crush, shouldering their way past the downtown shops, stopping to hug friends from out of town who visited just once a year.

The local citizens and even those who stayed behind in the Bush, who didn't have the funds to make the long journey to town, were equally enthralled by the world championship. Eskimos and Indians from all regions of the state, and whites too, shared a special feeling for the Rendezvous. The Natives considered the dog races an emblem of their culture and way of life. For the whites, raised on Jack London tales, dog races represented the mystique of the north country. Television didn't yet exist in the far reaches of Alaska, but the Rendezvous was a special event broadcast on statewide radio, and work and play stopped as people sat close to the big boxes. Such a vast land could not be tamed, but if only temporarily, it could be unified.

By 1958, the "Rondy," as it was affectionately and commonly called, was spawning its own legends and, in a remote state that had little sporting tradition, its own sports heroes.

Tough Earl Norris of Willow, who had driven a team of dogs carrying supplies for mountaineer Bradford Washburn's ascents of Mount McKinley and other Alaskan peaks, was the 1947 and 1948 champion. Gareth Wright won his first title in 1950, won again in 1952, and still again in 1957. Raymond Paul, too, won three crowns between 1951 and 1955, and Jimmy Huntington, of the respected Huntington clan in Huslia, won the 1956 championship.

Huslia is a tiny Athabascan Indian village near the Koyukuk River some eight hundred miles north of Anchorage. But its home-bred dogs sure could run.

Huntington was one of the early Huslia racers called the Huslia Hustler. People liked the sound of that. It rolled off the tongue in nice alliteration. In those days the nickname was applied to anyone from Huslia who was a fast musher. The fans weren't choosy. They didn't realize in 1958 that the nickname would henceforth become the province of one man and one man only.

Norris, Paul, Huntington—they were all well-known dog mushers in 1958 when twenty-four-year-old George Attla made the first visit of his life to the big city of Anchorage.

In the days leading up to the Rendezvous, the Anchorage newspapers and airwaves were filled with stories about the big race. There was speculation about whether Wright could defend his championship. There were nods to the prowess of the veteran Norris. There was mention of a newcomer named Roland Lombard, a veterinarian from Wayland, Massachusetts. He was a curiosity for having traveled so far—five thousand miles—for the race.

In the coming years, Alaskans would learn that "Doc" Lombard was far from being a mere curiosity. He would become one of the greatest of Rondy champions and the greatest of George Attla's rivals. The best champion in any sport is usually defined by the moments when he must be at his best. Great challengers push great champions to unsurpassed heights, especially if their rivalry spans years. Muhammad Ali had Joe Frazier to wring every ounce of skill from his body. Chris Evert had Martina Navratilova to battle for glory. And Attla had Roland Lombard to pressure him and challenge him and beat him. If Attla was even to dream of becoming the best of all time, he had to best Roland Lombard to make the claim.

That was all still to come, though. In 1958, when the mushers clustered in bars and the fans gathered in restaurants, drinking beer and coffee, none of them talked of George Attla. They had never heard of him. There was no reason they should have. He had never won a sled dog race in his life, not even in his own village.

But Attla was a competitor with motivation, with will and desire. Aching to prove that he could excel, Attla burned to demonstrate his abilities. This was his stage and his moment. The time had come for him to show the world that the tuberculosis that had wrecked his childhood, confined him to hospitals for years, wrenched him from his family, and resulted in surgery that had left him with a lifelong limp—was not enough to quell his spirit and prevent him from being a champion.

That was the untold story of George Attla at his first Fur Rendezvous. For the time being, it was his secret and his private motivation.

On the afternoon of February 21, 1958, the first time George Attla stood on his sled runners in downtown Anchorage, there was no way for the thousands of fans to know that within three days this man would be the toast of the state, that in future years he would come to be regarded as the greatest sprint dog musher of all time, and that beyond all that he would become a symbol not just of excellence, but of courage.

Back home in Huslia, in the Interior, at trapping camps dotting the land, friends and relatives had radios turned on and the volume turned up high. Though they were rooting for George Attla, few believed he could become a champion, and not a soul among them would have predicted that thirty-five years later he would still be racing. One of the most remarkable careers in all of sports was about to begin.

Chapter 2

Early Dog Days

You couldn't tell the century by the Attla family. In 1933, the year George Attla was born, the United States had long been an industrialized nation. There were skyscrapers of steel and concrete in the big cities. Americans drove automobiles to work.

Alaska was part of the United States, a territory three decades shy of becoming one of the fifty states. However, its northern reaches might as well have been part of the then-Soviet Union—so little did the area have in common with the New Yorks, Bostons, and Chicagos of the country.

The Athabascan Indians of the small villages along the Yukon and Koyukuk Rivers, and other of Alaska's Interior waterways lived the way their ancestors had lived for centuries. They were the indigenous people of the region. There were no factories, no cars, no roads even, where they lived. They knew little of these things. To support themselves, they hunted, fished, and trapped.

There are seven groups of Athabascans in Alaska sprawled across an area of several hundred square miles and encompassing both Fairbanks in the north and Anchorage in the southcentral region. Although small numbers of these Indians lived in Alaska's largest cities, the main concentrations of Athabascans were in the north, in small communities. Here there was no service industry because there was no one to serve. Tourism was a foreign concept then, too, in an area connected to the outside world by only Bush pilots and riverboat pilots. Few tourists in those days had the desire to travel north.

There was no supermarket in George Attla's neighborhood. If you wanted dinner, you went out and killed it. No one was going to deliver it, and there was no restaurant to patronize if you didn't feel like cooking. This was a true subsistence lifestyle—and it was not an easy existence.

The powerful Yukon, the largest of the big rivers of Alaska and the Yukon Territory, provided a continual supply of fish. Salmon and whitefish were the staples of the healthy diet for both humans and the ever-present huskies that earned their keep as work dogs, hauling wood for fires in winter and building materials in summer. The dogsled was the principal means of transportation.

The Attla clan was spending the summer months in fish camp, near the village of Koyukuk, about thirty miles downriver from the town of Galena, when George was born on August 8, 1933. Attla's parents, George and Eliza, had ten children—six boys and four girls. It was a year-round job to provide for so many hungry little ones, and indeed, as Eliza went into labor, family members were busy catching, cutting, and drying salmon into strips for the winter. George Attla's mother was aided in the birth by a midwife, Madeline Solomon, a family friend and a well-respected community figure who became famous for her efforts to perpetuate Native dialects among young people. There was no trained doctor for hundreds of miles in any direction.

At the time, the winter log cabin home of the Attlas was in a village of a few dozen people. Cutoff, as it was called, was in an area that frequently flooded, and state officials told the inhabitants they would not build a school there. If the families in the area would consent to establish a new village on higher ground, a school would be built at government expense.

The Attlas were one of the families that moved. The new community, sixteen miles to the south, was called Huslia, and about two hundred people settled in the vicinity. The school was a long time coming, and for a time only seven students attended.

The memories of George Attla's earliest years have dimmed in his mind, but what he recalls of his home life is pleasant. He remembers constantly playing roughhouse games with brothers Steven and Robert.

"Most of my childhood memories are about fish camp or at the trapping cabin," said Attla. "We never went to school at first. At home, all we spoke was Indian. We didn't know English." In modern-day Bush Alaska, the situation is reversed. Few speak the Native tongue, and English is a child's first language.

Today, Bush villages have cable television, insulated homes that are built against the elements, and snowmachines for winter travel. Modern machinery and conveniences, though, were unknown in the Native trapper's home of the Thirties and Forties. A man like George Attla, Sr., had to be a skilled hunter and fisherman to feed his big family. Despite daily hard work, there was no getting so far ahead that he could enjoy freedom from worry. By the standards of the Nineties, it was a hard life, but not a bad one for a growing boy with a lot of energy. It was a life spent outdoors.

"Compared to today," George explained, "we didn't know what we were missing. But we were never hungry, and we were always happy. We thought we had—well, we did have—everything we needed. We had plenty to eat, and we slept good. What more can you ask for?"

There were no freezers or refrigerators in Huslia. All the fish was dried. In the summer, the Attlas lived on what they dried or saved in the spring. That included muskrat, goose, and moose shot or trapped in the fall and winter.

George, Sr., was a crack shot. He couldn't afford to miss. He always got his moose. Alaskan moose can weigh twelve hundred pounds or more, and once the bone is trimmed away, a single moose can provide up to seven hundred pounds of meat. In early fall, George, Sr., hunted bears. Winter comes early in the far north, and that means the lakes and rivers turn to ice by the first week in October. The black bears have just retired for the long, harsh winter, fattened up on enormous quantities of sweet wild berries. George, Sr., would let them feast, then track them to their dens.

George remembers bear meat as being especially tasty in the fall, once all those berries got into the animal's system. "It's kind of a sweet meat," he said. "They taste very good."

There was plenty to eat if you could catch it—salmon, whitefish, pike. The Attlas blocked the slough near their log cabin in September at the winter camp and built a fish trap; the fish retreating from freeze-up in a nearby lake would swim right into it. Ten-pound whitefish, fifteen-pound pike, and big king salmon weighing forty pounds or more would fill the traps. Even in winter, on the occasions when the water wasn't frozen, George, Sr., would throw nets out and scoop up as many fish as he could.

"My dad used to get so much fish," said George. "Yet it seemed like he could never get enough."

He probably couldn't. Not only were the Attlas a large family, but it was understood in Athabascan villages that anyone capable would help out the elderly. Government programs to provide for senior citizens were nonexistent. A man or woman in his or her seventies relied on children and villagers. Families took care of families.

"If somebody wasn't able to go out and fish or hunt, then the people who were able went out and got meat and fish for them," said George.

In the winter, George, Sr., the expert hunter, turned into the expert trapper. Mink, otter, beaver, marten, wolf, wolverine, and lynx were all available in the area. Game was plentiful then in pristine areas rarely visited by human beings, areas where the rate of human invasion has increased noticeably over the years. Mink, in particular, were abundant, George recalls, and muskrat, too. "My dad's trapping area just had mink all over the place," he said. "There was a lot of mink. You go up there today and there's none left.

And muskrat. They used to get thousands of muskrat in the spring-time. There's nothing today."

One by one, as his boys grew older and reached the age of about seven, George, Sr., enlisted their help on the trap line. At first, the kids just rode with him and kept him company on the long rides on the sled. The farthest point away from the cabin on the trap line was about fifty miles. A trained racing dog team, pulling a musher and a lightweight sled, can go twenty miles an hour for short distances. A working dog team hauling a sled laden with equipment and two people clearly moved much slower. A trip up and down the trapline filled an entire day.

Covering long distances was simply part of living in the territory. Today, mushers traverse the country for pleasure, but in the days of Attla's youth, every dog sled trip had a purpose.

As the boys grew a bit bigger and stronger, at about age nine, they helped their father hitch up the dog team, then watched and learned as he placed his bait and set the traps.

George cherishes the memories of the bitterly cold mornings spent alone with his dad, learning how to care for huskies, how to space traps, and how to skin the animals. "That was a good time in my life," he said. By nature, though, George was not an early riser. His father, trained by years of responsibility and fueled by the knowledge that no one else would do the work if he didn't, went to bed early in the evening and rose in the middle of the night, perhaps at three o'clock, to prepare the provisions and to start loading up the sled for the day. A couple of hours later, he woke George and his brothers—with a struggle. On a morning of forty below zero, the boys preferred snuggling under the warm fur blankets. "'Are you guys going to sleep all day?' he yelled at us," said George. "It was five o'clock in the morning."

There were always husky dogs around fish camp, strong, hard-working dogs that could be relied on to help the family with its labor. Dogs were a key part of the operation. There were no highways for automobiles even if a family could afford one, and snowmachines hadn't yet made their way to the north country. To get anywhere in the winter, you could walk on snowshoes, or you could count on the dogs.

"The dogs were tough," said brother Steven Attla. "We were using them every day. They were definitely work dogs."

Bill Sturdevant, a long-time Attla friend, said younger mushers can't even picture the lifestyle of a Bush village decades ago. "It's a lost way of life now," he said. "Not completely gone, but close."

The Attlas kept a constant number of dogs, usually about sixteen. That was how many they needed, how many it took to get the work done, and how many they could afford to feed. On a typical trapline day trip, George, Sr., would harness up a team of ten dogs. Often, there was no trail to follow. The musher and the dogs would create their own, the dogs plowing through chest-deep snow to make their way. George, Sr., would cut out a trail and the going was a lot easier if it stayed clear, if the wind cooperated and didn't blow fresh drifts.

Marvin Kokrine, a generation younger than Attla, who grew up in the village of Tanana and later became a top musher, said the early days definitely toughened Attla.

"His ruggedness probably had a lot to do with the way he was raised," said Kokrine, "the way all the Athabascan people were raised in George's time. Very few planes went out there. There was no such thing as snow-gos."

Always, there would be a few dogs around the house for the kids to play with, and George loved his frisky playmates. He still owns pictures of some of the first dogs the kids had more than fifty years ago.

When he was ten, George was given the responsibility of breaking in six new pups, getting them used to a harness and pulling the sled. It took some time, but when the proud young man told his father he'd accomplished the task, the older man rewarded his son.

"He gave me two dogs," said George. "Oh, that was a big day

in my life. I remember those dogs. I was only ten years old, but they were my very own dogs."

Little did anyone realize how big a part dogs would play in the son's life. At that point, George was excited simply because he had dogs for trapping.

"Just before that," he said, "my father had given each of us our very own trapline around the cabin. We each had our own area. So, now I had my very own dogs, too.

"I can still remember when I caught my first mink. It was a couple of feet long. In a leg trap. I didn't use bait. I just set the trap on a trail. The first mink I caught, I never forgot it, because I went through the whole motion of taking care of it by myself. My oldest brother, Steven, was going to town, and I gave it to him to trade for candy and raisins."

Steven took the mink into Cutoff and made the deal his brother sought. That night, George climbed into his bed, slipped under the blanket to hide from his brothers, and ate all the candy and raisins.

The Attla family cabin was small and sectioned in quarters. The parents got the privacy of one quarter, a common section including the kitchen and dining areas made up another, and the last half was split between the female children and the male children. It was crowded. Beds were shared.

"We were all piled into one room at night," recalled Robert, one of George's brothers, who is two years younger. "We never had very much room."

The boys often made their own toys. They carved out small make-believe guns and boats. In summer, they pretended to be riverboat pilots, imitating the captains of the steamboats they saw gliding down the Yukon River. Other times they'd play at mushing dogs.

"Those are the only things we played, the only things we knew really," said George. "Riverboats, trapping, fishing, driving dogs. That was all that went on. That was our life."

George, Sr., was not a gabby guy. He favored the tactic of teaching his sons through example, of making them pay attention to what he did, rather than giving long-winded explanations. "He wasn't too much for words," said George. "He mostly showed us."

The first sled dog rides were not taken until the youngsters were old enough to comprehend what was going on around them. Yes, they were passengers enjoying time alone with their father, but they were expected to be observant passengers as they mushed along the trapline. Implicit was the directive: you, too, will be required to do this some day, so pay attention.

George, Sr., never told his son that, but he got the message. It wasn't until George grew up that he realized these fun trips in the woods were work for his father—very hard work. And later, when he was old enough to understand, George appreciated his father's hunting, fishing, and trapping acumen.

"We were always a season ahead," said George. A season ahead. That meant loading the kids onto a barge in the fall and ordering them to cut wood for the winter. The boys would cut enough wood for the main cabin and for the trapline camps, too. Then George, Sr., would haul a winter's supply of fish to caches along the trapline so he'd have food in place when he came back by dog team later in winter. He'd put salmon in place for the hungry dogs, too, protected in sturdy caches from any bears. When the snow fell and George Attla, Sr., returned to trap meat for his family, everything was in place. It minimized the time spent doing difficult tasks in forbidding weather, when the temperature dipped to sixty degrees below zero and the wind howled down from the North Pole.

"He worked at what he did," said George. "And he expected us to do our share of the work. Another thing. I don't remember my dad ever saying it was too cold, that he couldn't go out trapping. And believe me, fifty or sixty below is cold."

It is one thing to say you will stay indoors if you are a recreational musher, quite another if the welfare of your family is at stake.

George, Sr., worked hard training his dogs as well. They knew how to pull a sled, all right, but they could do more than that. The leaders were trained to hunt moose. They would chase down the big beasts, circle them, and essentially herd the moose toward the hunter.

"I have no idea how he trained them to do that," said George, still the admiring son decades after he saw the plan work. "But he could turn the dogs loose, and they'd bring a moose back. Or they would hold it till he got there."

Those same huskies would track black bears in the dens and lead George, Sr., right to them. It is not hard to see why George Attla would form a very favorable impression of huskies early in life. They could do anything—even play a child's game like hide-and-seek.

"Steven's dog would play with us," said George. "When he hid, we hid. When it was his turn to look for us, we all hid and then he'd look for us."

Chapter 3

Diagnosis: TB

In the summer of 1942, when he was nine years old, George Attla developed a problem. While he was playing with his brothers, and without warning, his right leg wouldn't straighten all the way. He tried to run and he stumbled. He thought he was just tired and achy from playing too hard. He was running a fever, too, but that didn't bother him very much. Kids usually ignore something like that. But one night, George was scared. He didn't understand what was happening to him, nor did his parents.

Everyone thought that with rest, the ailment would go away. Instead, it got worse. His leg wouldn't support him and he lost its full range of motion. If he had taken a fall, or bumped into something, it would be understandable. But no such event had occurred.

Even when he lay in bed, the leg stayed bent. It was as if it was deliberately spiting George's will. Instead of straightening out and returning to normal, the leg involuntarily folded up to his chest.

"I couldn't straighten it out," said George. "I tried and tried." Clearly, this was not a simple matter, and medical attention was needed immediately.

A worried George, Sr., bundled his son into a small boat and headed for the closest hospital, some two hundred miles away on the Yukon River in Tanana.

This would be the first time that young George was separated from his extended family and cabin home in Huslia. He was a fierce crier at that age, with powerful vocal cords, and sick and scared, he complained at the top of his lungs when his dad left him at the hospital alone and returned to the fish camp. George, Sr., could not afford to spend time with his son when the survival of the rest of the family was at stake. He was the provider. That was hard for the boy to understand.

George spent a month in the hospital. Doctors didn't give him much information, so he still didn't understand what was wrong with his leg. It was a lonely month of fear and worry, before his father came to pick him up.

George's recollection of that hospital visit—accurate or not—is that the doctors didn't do much to help him. They just got sick of this rambunctious child who was unhappy in hospital confinement and anxious to return home. So they discharged him. "They said I raised too much hell," George said.

The doctors shared their diagnosis only with George, Sr. Tuberculosis. Now rare, tuberculosis was a killer plague of enormous proportions nearly a hundred years ago. In the 1940s, despite advancements in medicine and medical care, it was still a debilitating illness. The prognosis for George was unclear: he would live, but unless the disease remarkably reversed itself, he would be crippled, unable to ever walk comfortably or to run easily again.

"It was a sad time for us," said Steven, George's oldest brother, ten years his senior. "At that time, people were still dying of tuberculosis. None of us knew what would happen."

While in the hospital, George was sustained by his memories of home. He thought frequently of playing with his brothers—especially the daring and naughty fun he had when he and his brother Frank stole smokes from their dad's limited tobacco supply.

The Attlas were not a rich family, so anything store-bought or obtained in trade for furs was closely accounted for. "If you had a carton of cigarettes," said George, "you *knew* you had a carton of cigarettes. If there were only nine packs left, you knew there were only nine packs left. My dad smoked his pipe and he had pouches of tobacco. It was easier to sneak tobacco than it was cigarettes.

"We had a smoking area—me, my brother Frank, and an Indian girl named Ishkishtak. I remember getting caught, and I got spanked by the old man. It was the only time I was spanked. I couldn't have been more than seven years old, but I was old enough to know better. At least he thought so."

George reminisced about the only time he was spanked by his mother, Eliza, too. He was about the same age, his mischief age. Eliza did bead work, and she had patterns she used for sewing and making mukluk boots. One day George and some of the other kids got into her patterns and started cutting paper dogs out of them. "By the time she got home, we had everything cut up," said George. "Oh, we had a huge dog team. And I can remember her whipping us then."

It is funny how even the moments that seem the harshest take on a special quality of warmth when you are far from home. Even the spankings sounded good to a boy marooned away from home and left alone in a sterile hospital environment.

When George returned home to Huslia, his leg never actually pained him, but it was never quite the same, either. He couldn't run the way he did before and he didn't have the strength to work with the dogs on his dad's trapline the following winter.

In the Athabascan culture, there were definite divisions of labor for men and women. The head of the household was the meat provider. The woman was custodian of the home.

Eliza did all of the cooking and sewing. She made the clothes and mukluks from the fur pelts her husband trapped. As a boy, George wore a winter coat made of rabbit skin, and his other outer garments were made from different furs and feathers. All the local families lived off the vast and isolated land that surrounded them. You could travel two hundred miles and not see another soul. There was no big city nearby where you could buy tailored clothing.

The climate was not unlike that of the Great Plains states. It was hot in the summer, with temperatures often reaching to ninety degrees, so thin layers of clothing were appropriate. But in the worst winter months, many heavy layers were needed to cope with the intense, dry cold of fifty below zero or so. So the women's work was essential to family well-being. Still, it hardly interested George. Like all Athabascan boys, he wanted to work alongside his father.

It was frustrating for a growing boy to be saddled with a physical problem. There was no real place for George. If he could not help his father and develop the subsistence skills he would someday need for his own family, then his only alternative was to do women's work. It was humiliating, but George helped out in the kitchen and around the house. He wasn't content. He wanted to resume the wild play with his brothers and participate with the same vigor he had before.

"When he came back," said Robert, "it was great. He was limited in what he could do, but he still overdid it. He would lay himself up, just exhaust himself."

But getting around on crutches made it difficult for him to keep up with his energetic brothers. Kids being kids, of course, they teased him about doing girls' jobs and then ran away so he couldn't catch up to retaliate. George got wise, though, and developed a method for getting back at them later.

In this way, the small cabin paid dividends for George. At bedtime, his brothers had to share the small bedroom with him.

"He might have been having problems with his legs," explained Robert, "but from walking around all the time on the crutches, he had built strength in his arms. Oh yeah, he got back at us. He'd whack us with those crutches."

One thing George had always enjoyed with his brothers was participating in foot races. The contest was to see who could run the farthest from the cabin and back through the snow without boots on—even on the coldest days of winter. Each boy carried a stick and placed his marker at the turnaround spot, the place he reached before he couldn't tolerate the cold anymore. George was a pretty fast runner when they first started playing the game. But when he returned home from the hospital, he couldn't go as far with his marker as he used to, and it was only then that he began to realize his leg might never be as good again.

The idea of becoming a dog musher, or an athlete of any kind, was never any further from reality than it was that year. Life, it seemed then, would always be very hard for this boy trying to get around in the woods on one reliable leg.

It was during the frustrating period immediately following George's hospitalization in Tanana that his father gave him the responsibility to train the litter of pups. It was something he could do while hanging around the cabin, something he could do to re-establish his worth. George, Sr., never said as much, but it was apparent his heart ached for his son trying to find his proper place in the scheme of things. The dogs were a gesture that would change the boy's life.

"George started to work with dogs when he was quite young," said Robert. "The dogs replaced his legs. He could do things with dogs that he couldn't do with his legs, even just playing around camp."

Chapter 4

Endurance

The leg only got worse. Little boys were born to run, not hobble, and George Attla did not take his inactivity well. He coped with the help of his family, but kindness could not cure tuberculosis.

The one curse of living in a tiny village was the lack of advanced health care. Even today, many Alaskans who live in the Bush must travel long distances for even the most rudimentary of medical treatment. And for any major procedures they must go to major population centers.

As George's leg gave him more and more difficulty, his parents realized he had to return to the hospital. This time, though, it would not be merely for a month-long stay. Twelve-year-old George moved to Tanana for about a year and a half. World War II ended while he was in the hospital.

Once again, George resisted being separated from his family, but he gradually adjusted to living in a hospital. There were many other children so he made new friends, and together they made the best of things. They were all sick, all removed from their families, all supporting one another. They went to school at the hospital, and this is where George learned how to speak English. It was not formal schooling, but he picked up the language in a rough way—a word here, a phrase there, understanding it better than he could speak it at first.

Time passed, but at no time does George remember doctors telling him exactly what his health problem was, or what his future would hold. Perhaps they simply figured a child couldn't understand. He knew he was in Tanana because of the stiffness in his right leg, but he didn't know exactly what was wrong. Nobody ever said, "You're here because . . ."

Since he had been in the hospital for a month the first time, George assumed he would be there for a month this time, too. He never imagined the hospital would become his second home, and as the months dragged on, there were times he thought he would never go home.

"After a while, I accepted it," said George. "I can remember some good moments there. I really learned a lot."

Still rowdy by nature and temperament, George took on all comers in fist fights. He loved the combat and thought he was pretty tough. Later in life, George would become a tremendous boxing fan who followed all the matches of Sugar Ray Leonard, George Foreman, and Mike Tyson. Young George beat back virtually all challengers and became unofficial champion of his hospital section.

"I'd whip the ward, you know," said George. "I enjoyed it. It was just the thing to do."

Attla couldn't whip anybody from a hospital bed, though. When he was put in traction to straighten out his right leg once and for all, he was in no position to throw jabs. Doctors put a pin through his knee and another pin through his heel and attached a weight. He was immobilized. Attla stayed on his back for a month and a half. That's when the other kids teased him. They knew he couldn't reach them to pop them, so they danced out of his reach. It was much the same as it had been at home when his brothers teased him, without the gratification of his bedtime revenge.

This was Attla's first lesson about being an athlete and staying in shape. Once he was removed from traction, he was placed in a wheelchair. He had mobility again, and his first thoughts were,

"I'm gonna get even with them." Bush living ensured a wiry, muscular build in Attla, one that he has maintained for his entire adult life. Play at home involved races and wrestling. Work at home involved endurance tests in the cold and heavy lifting. No one lay on his back for weeks at a time. No one could afford that kind of laziness.

But six weeks of lying in bed made a big difference. Attla picked a fight with one of the kids who'd been taunting him, one who had been an easy mark before he'd been placed in traction. Only now he couldn't outbox the same kid. "He beat the heck out of me." Attla's strength had ebbed away. He needed time to regain his conditioning.

"It was a lesson that I never forgot," said Attla. "I learned that if you didn't do something, that you were gonna get flabby and out of shape. That was really an important lesson in my life."

He never let himself get out of shape again.

The doctors never told George how he contracted tuberculosis—they may never have known themselves—or what it was. When he eventually realized on his own what disease he had, he became scared. He only knew one thing about tuberculosis—that whole families were known to die from it. Nobody in his immediate family struggled with the illness, but he heard the stories. No one at the hospital ever took the time to comfort the little boy or explain that he wasn't going to die. Only his mother and father made that effort. They told him it was important that he go to the hospital and that he would be taken care of there.

"I wasn't happy about it," said Attla. "I missed home. It was quite a big change, and the way of life was so different. But I didn't understand what was happening."

Doctors hoped that the prolonged period in traction would be the remedy for Attla's crooked leg. It was straight for the first time in several years when George returned to Huslia after eighteen months.

Still, he needed crutches to get around and, once again, it was hard to keep up with his playmates. He remembers one friend, Tony Sam, also a future dog musher, who tried to help Attla get around by tying cans to his crutches. That way the crutches wouldn't sink into the snow so deeply. But it didn't work.

"He used the dogs more to get around," said Steven. "He was always breaking his crutches, and he'd ride around with the dogs."

Attla's leg was supposed to improve to the point where he could assume the normal Athabascan lifestyle, but that did not happen. Instead, his leg weakened, and it slowly began to curl up again.

A year of life in the village passed, but Attla was further from being able to trap and hunt than ever before. And at age fourteen, he was old enough to realize that deterioration in his leg was likely to lead to more medical treatment.

"I was pretty disgusted with it by then," said Attla. "It was so hard to get around in the winter. I didn't even work much with the dogs. I was around the house with pretty much nothing to do. I was bitter."

More and more, the slender, tough, growing boy was counted on, not for trapping, but for women's work. It was the responsibility of the women in the family to make the fish nets in winter that would be used in fish camp the following summer. It was something George could do, too, without relying on his leg.

There was one way he could make himself feel useful as a manly hunter, though. As a youngster, George received a shotgun from his father. Now, even if he couldn't stalk most wild game, he could climb into a canoe and paddle down the river toting his gun. He sat in the canoe and shot ducks out of the sky. So he was a family meat provider in his own way.

"I was a pretty good shot," said Attla.

But that didn't make up for having to do the dishes some of the time, since his brothers let him know exactly where he stood. He felt their teasing much more keenly now as a slightly older boy than he had a few years before, when he thought his status was temporary. Now he wondered if he would ever fit in.

Even if George thought his future was cloudy, and he couldn't see past the immediate woes of the present, his father realized his son's future revolved around his well-trained dogs.

There were always village dog races at the end of the year during the holidays. The week between Christmas and the New Year was the time for the biggest gatherings. The Attla family traveled north the short distance to the village of Hughes, where they had annual races and dances.

The races ran between sixteen and twenty miles, out of the main street of the town and back, finishing in front of what seemed like big crowds, but couldn't have been more than a hundred people. The biggest cabin in town was twenty feet by twenty feet, and the whole village could fit inside at once for the festivities.

George, Sr., always brought a full team of ten or so dogs to race, and he chased the small prize money offerings. Side bets were made, too.

"That was one of the bigger events in the winter time when I was a kid," said George. "I never forgot those races."

It was the highlight of the winter. The men raced their dogs as much for bragging rights as for the money. The kids clustered down the hall from the dances to play games. One game involved gaining possession of a broom by pulling it away from another competitor. It was their version of a traditional game that even now is contested at the annual World Eskimo-Indian Olympics.

"We never got together often," said George, "so I remember it as being very exciting. Going to Hughes was like going to the big city for us. We didn't have schools to get together, so we only saw other kids from other villages on these occasions."

Sometimes that was how you first met your relatives, your cousins, and in later years, how you might meet your future wife.

George, Sr., won his share of races and developed a reputation as a knowledgeable dog man. Typically, one musher won the championship for a couple of years with the same dogs in his team. Then another musher would develop a team grown up from a new litter and would take over for a few years. Dog teams tended to run in cycles because the village mushers could only afford a handful of new dogs at a time. Today, the best mushers have dozens of young pups every year to choose from and train.

"There was no mass producing of pups," said George. "Whoever produced the best litter of pups in any given year would be the champion for a while. It was that way, too, when I started racing professionally. It was too expensive to do it any other way."

Many village mushers didn't even have enough dogs to field their own teams, so they pooled dogs with their friends. There were only a half-dozen mushers in the open class in Hughes in a given year, but the top dogs may have represented many households. This pooling technique became a staple of smart village mushers when they traveled to big races around Alaska, too. Robert Attla said there was no jealousy among the dog owners, because if one of their teams won, they all shared in the glory.

George was a wide-eyed boy at the village races. He loved what he saw, and it planted in him the idea that dogs could do more than haul timber or provide transportation on the trapline. They could be used for sport, too.

The one memory Attla enjoys above all others, one that helped sustain him through his illness, is his first encounter with sprint dog racing. George, Sr., was running the family team, but George was able to borrow three dogs from Lucy Sackett, a perennial winner in the women's class and mother of a future state senator, John Sackett. "I guess I got it in my head that she must have the fastest dogs," said Attla.

He entered Lucy Sackett's team in the junior race, which was less than two miles long, and at the age of eight, George Attla won the first race of his career. It was just for kids, not the kind of race that even shows up on a musher's lifetime record. But it remains special to him. It would be nearly seventeen years before he won another race.

Chapter 5

Lifeline

Bill Sturdevant was fifteen years old the first time he met George Attla in 1962. When Attla came to Anchorage to race, he often stayed in the Sturdevant home, his dogs making camp in the yard. Eventually, Sturdevant matured into a rival sprint dog musher, but the two men remained close. They shared stories and racing experiences over many years.

Once, George told Sturdevant that his aunt had supernatural powers. When he was stricken with tuberculosis, he visited her home. "She told him she would dream him into a way of life," said Sturdevant. That way, she advised George, would be through handling dogs.

Sturdevant is no skeptic. He believes Attla's aunt could make special medicine in this manner and he scoffs at anyone who ridicules the story. "If they can't measure it, weigh it, or take its temperature, then it doesn't exist," he said of mainstream white culture in the United States today.

The Athabascan culture was more spiritual. Indeed, Attla's aunt was prescient. There was no one who made a living from dog mushing at the time—it was a hobby for some—but she was proven right. Unfortunately, George also still had great need for another kind of medicine as well.

After his second hospital visit, Attla's life changed even more dramatically. Now fifteen years old, he was shipped to Sitka, more than one thousand miles south of Huslia, for more sophisticated medical care. There, George received treatment at the hospital and attended classes with other young Native kids at the Mount Edgecumbe School, a school of all grades through high school. It was here he realized that his knowledge of English was limited, and he got the chance to study and improve his second language.

George felt he was a misfit from the start in Sitka. Again, he missed his life in the secluded Bush. He was in a city of several thousand strangers in a climate that was much milder and damper. In the winter when it snowed at home, it rained in Sitka. And since he walked with a limp, he became an easy target for mean-spirited teasing. When he looks back on that time of his life, decades later, Attla recalls his roiling emotions. "That period of my life put a lot of chips on my shoulders," he said. "I realized I didn't fit in very well there. The Native kids from other villages had been exposed to more than I had. They spoke better English. Plus, they could read."

Attla wished he had his dogs Buster and Jimbo for friendship, but all he had for companionship was a picture of his two favorite huskies. He spent two years in Sitka, a major portion of it in the hospital. It was two more very long years, once again removed from family. More than once he wondered whether he had been forgotten. Back home, though, his brothers and sisters missed him.

"It was lonesome," said Rose Ambrose, one of George's sisters, who still lives in Huslia. "We were really a big, close family, and it was hard for one of our brothers to be away. When he first went, I'm sure he was pretty lonesome, too. He wasn't hearing any news at all from home. It was hard for him."

A thousand miles from their son, the Attlas found it financially impractical to visit. In addition, Sitka was not Athabascan. The city had been settled by Russian explorers, and although there were Alaska Natives there, it was essentially a white man's community. "People talk these days about how difficult it is to live in a white world and culture," said Rose. "For him, it was worse. He was so doggone mixed up. When he came back to us, it was like he came back from some other planet. He didn't understand his parents. He lost his language. It took a long time for him to learn the ways again."

At the hospital, the doctors decided that George's right leg would never straighten on its own and that if they placed it in traction again, he would likely just suffer another relapse. So they performed major surgery, fusing the kneecap. That made the leg permanently straight. Ever since, Attla has walked with a pronounced limp.

George spent long months in a hospital bed recuperating, with his only fresh air coming from open windows. He and some of the other kids made a game out of trying to trap seagulls, leaning out the window with handmade hooks baited with bread laced with ether. If the seagulls bit into the bread, they went to sleep and the boys reeled them in. They didn't keep or kill them, though. They were merely desperate for amusement.

Attla became friends with the hospital staff, and he made some good friends among the other children. Yet he became increasingly bitter about his leg, being marooned so far away from home, and eventually, about having fun poked at him by schoolmates once he began attending Mount Edgecumbe. "That was a tough time, I had a lot of anger."

The only communication with his family for nearly two years was through sporadic letter writing. "We would only hear from him every three or four months," said Steven. Attla went to school at Mount Edgecumbe because there was no money to bring him home right away. His lack of English skills led school officials to place him in classrooms with elementary school kids. Almost seventeen years old, he sat next to ten-year-olds. The experience left him scarred.

A boy who was then ill-equipped to fight back verbally, George challenged his harassers to fistfights. Maybe a boy with a stiff leg couldn't float with the speed of a Muhammad Ali, but a wiry, five-foot-eleven boy with strong arms could cope and adapt. Wilderness living was marvelous for that. George learned to be self-sufficient in Huslia and to deal with surprises thrown at him by changing conditions and a demanding environment. He developed his boxing skills, and by playing basketball regularly, he acquired a certain kind of foot speed that served him well in hand-to-hand battles. "For a kid that had one good leg, I was pretty quick," said Attla.

As hard as life was, there can be no doubt that the seeds of Attla's athletic determination had taken root by the time he left Sitka. He was angry, frustrated, and groping for his place in society. Yet, he was determined to make something of himself, determined to overcome what the world might see as a handicap.

When pushed and pushed hard by insensitive teenagers, young George did not shrink from their challenge. He pushed back, fought back. The character was there. Jim Welch, who is regarded as a sprint mushing expert of great wisdom, once traveled with Attla to a dog mushing symposium in Norway.

"Someone asked him from the crowd, 'How do you deal with being handicapped and still being able to race?'" said Welch. "He said, 'I don't consider myself handicapped.' Someone might say George always had a chip on his shoulder, but someone else might say that the chip on his shoulder is the driving force that made him a champion. I think he's used it as a tool. And as the years pass, I think he looks for other chips to motivate himself."

Motivation was not a problem for George when he returned home to Huslia after two years apart from his family. It was the early spring of 1951, and he was approaching eighteen years of age. He was hungry to establish a life for himself, but confused about just what to do. He had been through a difficult time in Sitka's alien environment, yet all the sweet memories of Huslia and fish camp that had sustained him seemed slightly askew when he returned.

Yes, he was happy about rejoining his family, but there were also many things he didn't look forward to. After all, before his hospital stay in Sitka, he had been relegated to doing women's work. Would it be women's work again when he got home? Or would he be able to create a more substantial role for himself in the village?

"At home, I was pretty happy for a while. It was good to be back with the family," George explained. "But when I went home, I didn't quite fit in there either. I was nearly a grown man by then, and I realized I didn't know how to hunt well. I wasn't a good hunter. I had missed so much."

It was good to be back in the flat open land, to watch the river move past in all its swirling power, to be close to the moose, the lynx, all the animals, and it was especially good to be back harnessing and running dogs. But even the old familiar routines were no longer so familiar. There was more city in George now.

Summer comes late to Alaska's Interior, so even after George had been home for a few months, winter still clung to the nights, freezing melting snow into crusty snow and small lakes and rivers into ice again. The Attlas began their migration to fish camp by traveling at night. Only George, now comfortable with a daytime schedule, was no longer used to staying up all night.

George was traveling with his brother Frank, but he became weary and stopped his dog sled to rest. He climbed into the sled basket and fell asleep. He woke up to find his outerwear was soaked. Time had passed, the temperature had risen, and without his careful guidance, the dogs had run the sled into a body of water. It was embarrassing to make such mistakes; carelessness in the wilderness is never rewarded and is often dangerous.

For a whole year, Attla felt somewhat out of place. He fished with the family during the summer, but not all family members were in fish camp. Some of his older brothers had already moved out and found their own fishing spots.

Although George, Sr., a man of few words, never explained to his sons that he saw an end to the lifestyle they led, he recognized that there would likely be big changes coming as Alaska's population grew and encroached on even its most remote regions. George, Sr., sent three of his sons to school at a Catholic mission in Holy Cross, a community a few hundred miles south along the Yukon River. "It was clear even then that the lifestyle might be slipping away," said Attla. "Really, in his mind, he could see that, so he was preparing the kids the best he could. He never mentioned why he would do these things, though. He just did them. I'm sure he saw what was coming."

Who knew better than George Attla, Sr., how hard it was to feed a large family?

George enjoyed being at fish camp again his first summer back, but when the hunting season arrived, he couldn't participate fully with the others. He had limited experience, and his leg was an obstacle. "It was hard for him to be out in the woods," said Rose Ambrose. "He couldn't just put snowshoes on his feet and chase after moose. He started using dogs in his hunting. The dogs were his taxi."

It always came back to dogs. Dogs, George thought, could be his lifeline.

Chapter 6

Last Place

In the years George had been away in hospitals, dog racing had grown in popularity in the villages. Races were scheduled more frequently, and the Fur Rendezvous World Championship had expanded.

People who lived hundreds of miles away in the Bush were taking an interest in the event, pooling the best teams in their areas, and putting their faith in a single musher to represent them. The men from Huslia set the pace and were the best.

When Attla returned to Huslia from Sitka, it was decided that he would try to make his living as a trapper. His only dogs were Buster and Jimbo, but his brother-in-law, father, and brother Frank each gave him a dog. So, suddenly he had a five-dog team.

Perhaps the entire sport of dog mushing would have been different if George Attla had become an accomplished trapper, but as he said himself, "I wasn't much of a trapper."

At first, George trapped with his father. Then he trapped on his own. There was one problem though: he didn't catch much. Even though he had been raised in the Bush and should have known all the secrets of the trade, Attla couldn't trap successfully.

"I really enjoyed it," said Attla. "I liked being out. I used to camp by myself a lot. In fact, I used to spend a couple of months by myself just living in a tent in the wintertime. I just wasn't a very good trapper, I never could figure out exactly why, but I couldn't trap worth a damn."

Attla knew trapping was supposed to pay the bills, but he also knew what was in his heart. "I wanted to race dogs," he said. "I was like any other kid."

The Rendezvous was a topic of discussion. Now it was something to dream about, to aspire to, the way a young boy growing up in New England might dream of playing baseball for the Boston Red Sox.

Once, George was out trapping with his brother Steven some fifty miles from home, and they brought a radio to listen to the North American Open Championship, the second biggest sprint mushing championship behind the Rendezvous.

That year, George had good reason to be interested. Bergman Sam, his first cousin from Hughes, was racing using one of Steven's dogs as one of his leaders. Sam finished third in the race. That's when the race became personalized.

"I told George, 'You know, we can do the same thing,'" said Steven. "That's where he got the idea to start racing. I really supported him at the beginning. I thought it would be good for him. It would give him the opportunity to excel at something. I was really surprised at how quick his success came in the big races, though. You couldn't predict that."

Quick, in this case, is a relative term. It would be overly simplistic to imply that Attla was inspired by listening to a race on the radio and became a winning dog musher overnight. He worked about five years trapping and doing other seasonal odd jobs while developing his mushing. One summer he worked as a deck hand on a tug barge for Jimmy Huntington, who also became a champion musher. It was just one of many odd jobs Attla would hold in the coming years to supplement his income.

Since a man had to make a living any way he could in the Bush, he could not afford to keep dogs that weren't hard workers, those that didn't have a future. Money was always tight, and the first priority was feeding the family. Dogs were extra mouths to feed, so any dog that didn't work and didn't fit in the plans was killed.

Life in rural Alaska in the Fifties was quite different from American life today. You couldn't give a dog away; no one would take it. If a dog was no good to you, it was of no value to anyone else, either. It was necessary to cull the dog team, choosing the best dogs for yourself and attempting to provide a painless death for the others. "I only thought two of the five dogs I had were any good," said Attla, "so I shot the other three. That's the way things were. No family kept extra dogs. It was a harsh thing to do and that might seem strange now, but it was the way things were done then."

Today's full-time dog mushers have dozens of dogs in their kennel, even hundreds, and any dog bred by George Attla today brings a price of several hundred dollars or more. "Out of the dogs in my kennel today," said Attla, "I bet my dad would have shot over half of them when he was running his trapline. Now people take them as pets if they are no good as racers. But not back then. It sounds pretty cruel, but you didn't keep anything extra. Only the tough ones survived."

That was the natural order of things in a subsistence lifestyle–for the people as well as the dogs. Only the tough ones survived.

When he first started racing, Attla had to raise a team from nothing. The money he made in the summer was earmarked for buying new dogs, though after this first year being left with only two dogs, his father's generosity helped. George, Sr., gave him a litter of pups. George's team was up to seven dogs for the winter of 1953.

But, once again, he had middling success. That winter, Attla was again a trapper, capturing otters and using his team for transportation.

But by the next winter, Attla entered his first adult race. Huslia had a big twenty-mile race on New Year's Day and Attla wanted to race in the open men's class. Since his dogs weren't old enough to compete, he borrowed his father's team.

The inexperienced Attla didn't have a strategy planned and didn't even recognize how fast was fast, which is why he was receptive to any advice or help he could get from a friendly source. He drew starting position number one and was excited. Jimmy Huntington was starting right behind him. George, Sr., took his son aside and recommended a cautious approach to feel out the experienced racer. Go fast in this stretch of trail, he said, and slow here.

However, George was living with his brother-in-law, Georgie, at the time, a great kidder. "George," he said, "I can tell you how to do this race. The secret to going fast is in the tow lines." George, Sr.'s sled was set up more for trapping than for racing, and Georgie told Attla that he would gain a tremendous advantage if he cut the lines short.

Shortening the lines would shrink the space between the dogs themselves and the sled. Georgie convinced his naive brother-in-law that they did it differently in the North American race. George believed him and cut all the lines, ruining them for future use. That in itself was a mistake, since good rope was costly and hard to find. Never mind, too, that George, Sr., was an expert and that these were his dogs.

"I was just like any other kid," said Attla. "I was thinking, 'What the hell does he know about it? He doesn't know what he's talking about.' I thought that I knew how far the dogs could run and how much you could push them. I thought I knew what I was doing with the dogs. But as soon as I took off, I realized I didn't know. The dogs were too close to each other. They were afraid to stretch out their legs because they thought they'd jump on each other. They were on top of each other. They couldn't run."

Robert Attla remembers that race well. "When Dad tried to advise George about dogs, he wouldn't listen," he said. "He listened to his friends first. He lost a race he should have won."

George, Sr., had advised Attla to run the dogs at a good pace for all twenty miles. George never did that on a trapline before, so he didn't know if the dogs could stand it and he didn't want to burn them out. "I was scared to push them," said Attla. "I had a five-minute lead, but it wasn't too long before Jimmy Huntington caught me and passed me."

Attla finished near the back of the pack of the racers. It was a public humiliation for him and, more significantly, an important lesson. It might be expected that George, Sr., would berate Attla; George knew he deserved to be told off. But his father never said a word about his mistake once he saw the shortened tug lines.

"I think he thought to himself, 'Well, that ought to teach him something,'" said Attla. "He must have thought I figured out that I'd made a mistake by myself. I remember it quite clearly. I realized that the old man knew what he was talking about and I learned not to listen to my brother-in-law. Georgie knew that I didn't know what he was talking about. He was just getting a big laugh at my expense. I wanted to cry."

It would have been easy for Attla to get angry, to be bitter about the manner of his defeat, but his disappointment passed quickly, and the educational aspect of the experience stayed with him.

"I decided I wanted to win," said Attla.

Building a good dog team with limited resources is a painstaking and often frustrating business. A good musher can put together a good team using his judgment and expertise, but he can't get anywhere without good dogs. And in the early to mid-Fifties, Attla was poor. Not so poor he didn't have enough to eat, but not rich enough to travel around buying dogs, weeding out the good ones from the bad ones.

The Attla kennel—if it can be called a kennel—consisted of only eight dogs the next winter. They were eight fine dogs for running a trapline, but still did not guarantee winning race results.

Sprint dog mushing was in its infancy, and dogs were still almost exclusively used as work animals. But, for the first time, Attla decided on his own to experiment with some training procedures. Of course, he didn't have the time to take only training runs, but he made the dogs run more often and longer distances as they worked the trap lines. He also made them go faster.

A year later, Attla focused on making a good showing at the village race in Hughes. This was Bergman Sam's era, and his large family owned many dogs and was intensely interested in racing. He was his family's designated driver.

Attla concentrated on beaver trapping that winter, and the beavers were plentiful. The season ran from January to March with a limit of twenty beavers, but, for once, Attla scored a major trapping success and quickly caught his limit. He used all his free time to run his dogs and train for the Hughes race. He had six of his own dogs and borrowed two of his father's finest. No doubt George, Sr., decided his son was going to be a smarter racer than he had been back home.

"My father never said much to me about my racing dogs, but I got the idea that he liked it," said Attla. "I think he sensed how important it was to me to be able to do something well. I wasn't that easy to get along with back then. I still had that chip on my shoulder. I wanted to prove that I could do something as well as any man there. The only way I could do it was with the dogs. It was clear it wasn't going to be trapping. He could see I wasn't worth a damn trapping. I had a lot of fun doing it, but that wasn't my thing."

The scars from George's rough childhood were still very visible and not only in his unusual gait. He lost his temper easily and for little reason. "I would fly off the handle," said Attla. "I still didn't feel that I fit into that world. It was because I wasn't as successful as the other guys my age in the village. I was still trying to find a way to make my place. I wanted to be special at something."

The improvement came slowly in dog mushing. George picked up pointers from his dad, his brothers, his friends, but he didn't have the forum, the team, or the equipment to prove himself. This time, though, Attla sensed he had a pretty good team. When Bergman Sam saw Attla's team, he told George that he thought his dogs were potentially good enough to win the Hughes race.

"I believed him," said Attla. "It looked like it to me. We'd go out driving together, and he'd drive his team, and I'd drive my team. My dogs could outrun his."

It is about ninety miles from Huslia to Hughes, and there was heavy snow that year. The only way to get there was to drive the dogs, but the snow was so thick that Attla himself had to break much of the trail on snowshoes, stomping out a path in front of the dogs. The journey took four days.

Attla viewed the Hughes race as his big chance to make an impact on his peers. He was nearly twenty-one years old, though, and he'd led kind of a sheltered life. There were few eligible women in such a small village as Huslia, but at a big spring carnival, a non-stop party like this, people came from all over. It was an end-of-winter celebration, a joyful release. The trapping season was over, and there was a lull before the fishing season began. Soon the rivers would break up.

But, it turned out, there were other lessons to be learned before Attla could become a mushing champion. The flirtatious, eligible young women in Hughes certainly caught Attla's attention. He'd trained long and hard in the Bush, but once he got to the village he forgot all about his dogs. There were three girls who moved together in a group, and they all looked beautiful to him.

"All that damn work," said Attla. "I must have put two months into training those dogs and I gave it all up to chase those girls."

The girls were from Allakaket, another village in the area, and they were blushing at George's attentions. He was very bold in his pursuit of them, making his interest no secret, and that provoked the ire of an old woman.

"I was really rugged," said Attla. "I didn't pay attention to what anybody told me, you know. I walked my own line. This old lady came up to me as I was coming back from the outhouse one morning and bawled me out. She lectured me about chasing these three girls."

The old woman's message was simple: she told Attla that he

would regret this kind of behavior later in life. She warned him that as he matured and grew older he would feel remorse over such foolish and rude activity.

"Right at that moment, it didn't mean anything to me," said Attla. "But when you get old, you do think about those things. It's true. If you did something in your life, it stands out when you get older. You remember some of those things better than you do the happy moments. She was right."

Attla partied hard that week, drinking and carousing, and he was trounced in the race. He had violated the first rule of dog mushing—take first-rate care of the dogs, and take care of the dogs first.

"I just completely blew that race," he said. "I was too busy partying. I didn't take care of my dogs the way I was supposed to, feeding them, bedding them down. By the time the races started, they were way overweight. My dogs had been lying around for a week and had just blown up, they were so fat."

The dogs had been idle for too long, and they were not race sharp. In fact, the night before the race, three of them broke loose and spent hours running around the village. They stole food and became bloated. The same description fit the boss as well, and the Attla team finished last.

"I think that was one of the best lessons of my racing career," said Attla, "It never happened again. As much as I partied after that, I understood that the number one thing was to take care of my dogs."

All athletes must develop their skills. No competitor is born with all the knowledge he needs. There was value in this failure for Attla if it helped him progress. And it did.

Chapter 7

A Break

George Attla first realized he could become a good dog musher, not when he actually won a race, but when he saw someone else lose one.

Raymond Paul of Galena was a prominent musher in the early Fifties. He won his first World Championship title in 1951 and the big Anchorage event in 1954 and 1955.

In the spring of 1955, after he had captured his championships, Paul returned to the north country for the spring carnival racing. The village racers in Huslia, Hughes, and all around the region were demonstrating a growing interest in mushing. They were experimenting with training and making plans to attend the big races themselves.

To Attla and his friends, Paul was a legend. He must have the best dogs because he was winning the big races, right? Maybe. Those dogs had never raced head-to-head against other village dogs.

Paul was a celebrity of sorts. He was from the same area and he was beating all comers in Anchorage. But the local mushers weren't in awe of him. They wanted to win. In what has become a tradition, local mushers picked Paul's brains for advice, then tried to beat his brains out on the trail.

Attla was in the race, and though he improved on his finish

since he didn't waste so much time partying, he didn't contend for the title. But neither did Paul. Three local mushers pulled ahead, mushers who Attla thought were beatable. They were in his class, as far as he was concerned.

"I thought I could beat them," he said. "And then they beat Paul. I knew he was doing well in the Rendezvous and the North American. I'll tell you, it was like turning a light on. I thought, 'Wow, my dogs are good enough to beat the guy who's the World Champion.'"

Thinking something and making it real, of course, are very different things. Many athletes have great confidence, but they never prove themselves. Attla was one of those guys. But now it was time for him to make something happen.

Attla got a break.

Paul was flying out, back home, but there was only room for four of his dogs on the plane. So he asked Attla, a good friend, to hook his remaining four dogs into his own team and drive them back to Huslia. The trip made an impression on Attla.

"They were better dogs than anything I had," he said. "As good as I thought my dogs were, these were superior to the dogs I had. They were just amazing."

Paul's dogs were well-trained huskies with experience. They could sense open water. They responded quickly to commands. These dogs were a step up in class for Attla, and it showed him what it would take to step up in class himself—permanently. Until he's taken the steering wheel of a Cadillac, a man might think his Ford is fine. But once he feels the difference, his desire to make a change might become an ache in his soul. Attla couldn't stop raving about Paul's dogs.

"Their minds were so good," he said. "They were much stronger and more willing than my dogs."

Right then Attla knew that he would have to get better dogs if he ever hoped to compete on a world-class level. And by now, with little experience and little success, he knew where he wanted to go ultimately. The idea of racing in the Fur Rendezvous in Anchorage and in the North American in Fairbanks was taking hold.

"It was something that was starting to take shape," he said, "but it wasn't anything I ever told anyone else. For the time, it was just my secret."

The trip back to Huslia was educational to Attla, but an amusing incident followed. He had possession of the dogs for close to a month, and in that time one of Cue Bifelt's dogs came into heat. Attla let Bifelt breed one of Paul's top-notch dogs with his female, and the result was a litter of pups that became champion dogs. So Bifelt owed Attla a favor, something that could come in handy later when mushers pooled dogs for the big races. One of the pups was so good that, as a nine-month-old, it raced all three days of the North American for Bifelt. Usually, the prime racing age for sprint dogs is two years and up. But this pup was a prodigy.

Attla was starting to recognize the qualities of a good dog. He participated in more village races, never winning, but moving up to third or fourth position. His brother Steven had a first-rate team, though, and frequently won races.

As important as it was to Attla to learn about Paul's dogs, his most significant experience in Hughes was meeting the woman who became his wife.

The first time he ever noticed Shirley Oldman, she was washing dishes at the kitchen sink of her home in Hughes while George was sharing a drink with her father, Abraham. Attla remembers being quite impressed with Shirley's figure as she labored.

Shirley was only sixteen years old, but when the carnival ended, she went back to Huslia with George. He was going on twenty-two and had discovered creative ways to make a living in summers that took him out of fish camp. That summer he worked in a mine. He also worked with a demolition crew tearing down a bridge, and as an iron rigger putting up the replacement bridge.

Summers were just necessary intermissions, however, in Attla's quiet pursuit of becoming a renowned musher.

"My own team was not improving that much, even though I was learning a lot," he said. "The quality of the dogs just wasn't there yet. That year, in 1955, Steven gave me one dog, and it was probably the best one I had, so you can see I wasn't really getting anywhere on my own."

Attla raced all winter. He felt he was getting better, yet he wasn't finishing higher. He was in a rut. What he could see clearly, though, was that he could compete. In 1956, Jimmy Huntington won the World Championship, and Bobby Vent, from Huslia, finished second.

"So, by then we knew we had the best dogs," said Attla.

In a way, George was trapped by the excellence around him, like an American swimmer or track and field athlete who finds his biggest challenge is making the United States Olympic team. Often, it's a certainty that he will win an Olympic medal if he can just qualify for his own nation's team. Similarly, Attla couldn't win any races in the small villages of the Interior, but he knew that if he could get a slightly better team and make the trip to one of Alaska's major population centers, he could do well. But for the time being, he was stuck in the minor leagues.

What was so remarkable was the fact that many of the very best sprint mushing dogs in the world were headquartered in a village of only two hundred people—something owed to the lifestyle of the area.

"I don't know how it happened," said Attla, "but really, our knowledge, the information on how to run dogs, was shared. If someone knew something about dogs that I didn't, he told me about it. Really, the whole village worked together."

It seemed just about any knowledgeable dog man from Huslia could win the big one if he could only get the chance. Bergman Sam promptly followed the example of Huntington and Vent by winning the North American in 1957. George Attla burned for his chance, too, but it seemed he had little power to make it become reality.

When a champion looks back at his life, he often can pinpoint a critical moment—a crossroads—when a decision or a choice made all the difference. The winter of 1957 was such a time for Attla. Up until then, he made only incremental improvements in his dog team, despite his five years of effort. He wondered if he would be forever doomed to the obscurity of his village, a musher only in the smallest of places, far from the spotlight.

If Attla was to get a chance, he would need some help, which is how Sidney Huntington came to play a pivotal role in George Attla's life.

Chapter 8

Village Advantage

Even as a child, George Attla respected Sidney Huntington. Though Huntington was eighteen years older than George, he earned Attla's admiration through his commonsense talk and his subsistence skills.

Huntington later became a statewide figure who served Alaska for nearly two decades on the state Fish and Game Board. He retired from that role at age seventy-seven in 1992, but was already a respected village leader by the time Attla returned home from his long hospital stays.

Huntington was close to the Attla family and was grateful to George, Sr., for his trapping advice.

"I learned a lot of lessons from George's dad," said Huntington.

He watched the young man struggle with his identity and sympathized with his attempts to make a meager living trapping.

"When he came back from the tuberculosis ward, he was trying to make things go," said Huntington. "He was young and restless, though, and having trouble."

Huntington, with foresight much in the mold of Attla's father, realized that running a trapline, as George did, might not offer the most secure future for the next generation.

"The competition for wildlife resources was pretty tough," said

Huntington. "Ninety percent of the people who lived in the Bush made their living off the animals. But there's room for just one person in a given area."

Like any man who spent a lifetime in the Bush, Huntington could be considered a dog expert. However, his brother, Jimmy, was the prominent racer of that generation of Huntingtons. And he remained so until Carl Huntington, Sidney's son, became the only musher to win the Fur Rendezvous World Championship in sprint racing and the eleven hundred-mile Iditarod Trail Sled Dog Race in the Seventies.

For some reason, one he can't even explain today, Attla never confided his dream of becoming a mushing champion to his father. He thinks, perhaps, he just wanted to show his father he could do it on his own and give him a reason to be proud. But he didn't want to make announcements. His brother Steven understood his longing, but even before any mushing discussions with Steven took place, Sidney Huntington became Attla's confidant.

It was at Christmas of 1957, Attla recalls, when he told Huntington that he thought he could compete with any of the other village mushers and make a good showing in Anchorage—if he could just find the right dogs.

Huntington had already observed George and felt he had a special kinship with the dogs: he brought a keen understanding of their nature to their training, and he could coax the best out of them. Over the years, that became a common observation among fellow mushers and competitors. They marveled at Attla's instincts with huskies much in the same manner as a coach in another sport will be admired for squeezing unexpected victories from a team that many think has only limited talent.

"It has always been apparent that George has had a gift with dogs," said Jim Welch, the Anchorage-area musher who purchased his first huskies from Attla in 1977.

"I'd heard about him, of course, but when I was trying to get started I met him for the first time. I was looking to buy some dogs and I ended up buying five dogs from George. They were the first real sled dogs I had. I figured his second-best dogs would be better than anyone else's best dogs."

Just because they were George Attla dogs.

It is not always easy to pinpoint what gives an individual a special ability to succeed and excel at a chosen sport. How do you do that? is a common question asked of sportsmen by sportswriters. Sometimes the player or coach can explain and sometimes he can't. Sometimes the outside observer can tell with a glance that he is witnessing something unusual, yet not be able to clearly define what it is he's seeing.

But it was Sidney Huntington who recognized George's potential first. "He looked like he was a person who could handle dogs," said Huntington. "I told him that. I also knew that money was pretty scarce around the trap line. The best you could hope to make then was fifty or sixty dollars a week. So mushing seemed like a good idea for him."

Huntington was gratified when Attla told him he was anxious to pull together a first-rate team and race in Anchorage, but he also knew George had never before won a race. He wasn't sure at first how a venture with George would turn out. And, of course, there was a major problem with finances. Attla figured it would cost six hundred dollars to get himself and his dogs to Anchorage and pay their expenses once in the city. That was a lot of money just to get to the starting line.

Huntington wasn't in a much higher tax bracket. However, he was a better and more experienced trapper than Attla. And he wanted to see Attla make good, wanted to see the village of Huslia get some glory. He told Attla that if he could get a competitive team together and get it ready to run, he would make sure money didn't hold him back.

"He told me to go ahead and train and see what I came up with," said Attla.

To do that, others had to be brought in on the plan. Attla

made his intentions of building a team known among dog men in the village. He borrowed four top dogs from Cue Bifelt. He got another dog on loan from his brother-in-law, Georgie. And he got a quality leader named Tennessee from Steven.

"Steven gave me the leader I wanted," said Attla. Tennessee boosted not only the caliber of the dog team, but the musher's confidence.

One advantage Attla had was the racing experience of the other villagers. Men who had raced in the big time and knew what it took were all around. "I was always into dogs, just training them," said Attla. "Even the dogs that weren't very good. But I hadn't ever trained dogs for three days of twenty-five-mile heats before. I was training them to do what I thought they had to do, but if I didn't know something, I could always go to someone in the village and ask them."

If a dog seemed ill or out of sorts, he could ask for help. If a dog developed a limp, he could ask. If a dog wouldn't eat, he could ask. If a dog didn't seem quite fast enough to keep up with the others, he could ask. "Somebody," said Attla, "would always have an answer."

During the winter of 1957, Attla didn't go trapping at all. He devoted all his time to training the dogs. These dogs ran more miles than trapline dogs. They ran more often. And they ran faster. Attla fine-tuned their abilities. There were no distractions. Every morning he would harness them up at the cabin, and the dogs would bound off into the trees. The sled runners made delicate whooshing sounds as the blades sliced through the snow. The temperature was often forty degrees below zero, and the dogs thrived on the work, pulling the musher standing on the back of the sled through the crisp air, their tongues wagging, their paws gripping the firm snow, their sleek muscles developing every day.

One day Huntington was trapping for beaver at a nearby lake when he saw Attla out training the dogs. He saw from a distance

George's powerful team moving at a gallop. The wind was blowing into their faces, but it seemed to make no difference.

"Hmm," Huntington thought. "They're going at a pretty good clip."

He guessed the sled was moving twelve miles per hour into a stiff headwind. That's when he became a true believer in Attla's quest. After seeing that workout, Huntington took George aside.

"I told him, 'If you take good care of the dogs, you shouldn't have much of a problem,'" said Huntington. "He didn't want to believe me."

It wasn't so much that Attla didn't want to believe him. More likely, he didn't want that belief as a distraction. This was the chance he'd pursued, and it might be his only chance. Yes, George thought he could win, but for an unknown from Huslia, overconfidence would have been a ridiculous problem going to Anchorage.

Still, Attla needed Huntington's faith. Periodically, he would mush out to Huntington's trapping camp and put the dogs on display for him, show him what they could do.

"And he told me he thought I could do it," said Attla. "He encouraged me. He believed in me."

This was not a universal feeling in Huslia at the time. After all, George hadn't truly succeeded at much that was important to the Athabascan people. He could speak English better than most, but that was of little importance at home. He had seen other parts of Alaska, but that provided little status, either. If anything, those two broadening experiences were obstacles to his becoming an accomplished member of the community. They meant only that he had to spend so much time readjusting to the ways that were second nature to his neighbors.

There was little evidence of greatness, either, in Attla's hunting and trapping, or even in his mushing, since he wasn't winning local races. So, why would everyone think he could compete and beat the best sprint mushers in the world in Anchorage?.

Attla has no memory of others insulting him, of telling him his aspiration was foolish, or of telling him he was wasting his time. But he suspected that's what most people in Huslia thought or were whispering. "Plus, I had one stiff leg," he said.

Again, there were no taunts, no one challenging Attla by suggesting he could not possibly become a winner because of his awkward stride. They did not tell him he would lose because he couldn't run as fast behind his sled as other mushers. But he could read it in their tone of voice, or read the skepticism in their eyes.

"In my mind, it wasn't a problem," said Attla. "I got used to it. I just adjusted to the way my leg was. By then, I didn't even know I had a problem. It didn't hurt me and it didn't bother me. But I knew there had to be doubts there. The whole village had a stake in a musher going to Anchorage because the dogs were shared. In a way, I was representing them."

Maybe, Attla said many years later, it was naivete that led him to think he could become world champion without ever becoming the champion of Huslia. It did sound crazy. But the combination of desire, the need to succeed and prove himself to his people, and an unshakable belief in the ability of the dogs kept Attla's spirits high as he prepared for the Fur Rendezvous.

"I didn't really know what I was getting into," he said. "But the only reality to me was that I could do it because of the dogs. Four of those dogs were the main dogs in teams that, over the last couple of years, had won the North American. And the others I had borrowed were equal to them. So it was almost like the dogs were saying, 'We're winners. We're as good as they are.'"

For several years, Attla had been convinced that first-rate dogs were all that stood between him and first place. Now he had the opportunity he'd ached for and he knew that the journey to Anchorage and his performance in the Rondy might very well be the most critical trip and race of his life. "This was the chance," he said.

There might never have been another one. What those dogs did in Anchorage, what George Attla did in Anchorage, in February 1958, redefined his life.

Chapter 9

World Champion!

Anchorage is a modern city in the middle of the frontier. With its paved streets and surprising traffic jams, tall buildings and tidy shops, it is as different from an Interior Alaska village as its weather is from Miami's.

A young Native coming to the city for the first time could be overwhelmed by its size, feel lost in its vastness, and, during the Fur Rendezvous, might easily be distracted by the swirl of activity.

But George Attla had been to spring carnivals before and sampled all of the many distractions; this was merely spring carnival on a grand scale. If a musher kept his mind on business, he would be fine. Some lessons stick.

Simply getting to Anchorage was part of the adventure for Attla. He and his dogs flew from Huslia to Fairbanks more than two weeks before the races. That made a dent in the expense fund he'd amassed from Steven, his parents, and Huntington. He stayed there and trained for several days with Harold Greenway, an old friend Attla met at the Mount Edgecumbe School who also became a winning musher. "When he saw my dogs running," said Attla, "he said, 'You could win the Rendezvous with those dogs.'"

Another vote of confidence.

He had a short period of worry, though, when it seemed his dogs were losing weight. Sprint dogs are lighter than long distance dogs, and the prime weight for a fast dog is estimated at forty-five to fifty pounds. In the Fifties, though, there really was no commonly used method to weigh dogs in the Bush, and Attla figured his dogs' weights on feel alone. He would lift them up and decide whether they were too heavy or too light to race. Loss of weight usually meant loss of appetite, and loss of appetite usually meant a dog was sick. But then the dogs started gaining their weight back, and Attla was relieved. He would have felt very silly if he'd had to scratch from the Rendezvous without crossing the starting line.

Attla still had to get to Anchorage, which is 360 miles south of Fairbanks by highway. Growing up in Huslia, there had been no need to learn how to drive, and Attla didn't have a driver's license, but he still somehow wangled the loan of a new truck out of a Fairbanks dealership. Young George talked as fast as he mushed, it seemed.

The vehicle was great looking, but it didn't have room to transport dogs. So Attla made a temporary trade with his friend Bill Carlo, and drove off in a pickup truck fitted with a plywood dog box. Attla got in a two-truck convoy with Greenway, also headed to the race. Things went smoothly until about ninety miles north of Anchorage, where the drive shaft broke on Attla's truck. If he hadn't been traveling with Greenway, George might have been stuck by the side of the road for a long time. Instead, he loaded his dogs in with Greenway's—they had twenty-four of them all together. But Greenway was driving with a friend, so there was no room for George in the cab. He rode with the dogs. A cramped fit, a noisy ride, but at least it was a ride.

"I remember piling in there," said Attla. "And that place was damned hot, really stuffy."

This was Attla's first visit to Anchorage. Though he retained his focus on the race, the bustling city and the four days leading up to the start left him pretty wide-eyed. He parked his dogs in a friend's backyard where they were well taken care of, so he had some time to enjoy the experience.

"I was pretty excited about the whole thing," said Attla. "There's a lot of excitement about the race, the whole atmosphere."

The musher everyone was talking about was Gareth Wright, the defending champion from Fairbanks. If Attla was mentioned at all, it was only in passing, when lists of entries were noted in the newspaper.

But the mushers, who had come from all over, including future champion Roland Lombard from Massachusetts, frequently got together to eat and drink. They stuck together walking through town, watching the people, shopping for souvenirs, enjoying the scene.

Between the air travel, the truck breaking down, and eating, the six hundred dollars Attla started his trip with was down to about twenty dollars.

"I was just about broke," he said, "and that six hundred dollars was supposed to get me all the way back home, too."

As if he needed any more incentive, it wouldn't hurt Attla any to earn the $1,500 cash prize for first place. In later years, the Fur Rondy purse grew significantly, sometimes paying the winner 10 times that amount. In 2000, race prize money totaled $60,000. But back then, $1,500 was a great deal of money to Attla.

"I didn't have any doubt in my mind that I could do it, though," he said. Gareth Wright was the favorite before the race started. Thousands of people lined Fourth Avenue in downtown Anchorage to catch a glimpse of the champion. Major sprint races are contested in major population centers, of course, because thousands of racing fans will not travel to small villages in the Bush to support and watch a race. They pretty much ignored underdog George Attla, and he did his best to ignore them, too. He had never seen so many people in his life, and if he stopped to think about the yelling, cheering throng, he might have trembled.

The dogs were another matter. Huskies spend most of their lives with other huskies and being driven by a musher whose voice, commands, and touch become familiar to them. They respond when spoken to, react quickly when they mush through the winds. However, more than ninety percent of the time they run, they run in solitude. They encounter few other dog teams, few other mushers, and few spectators other than the occasional curious skier, trapper, or snowshoer out along the trail.

If a musher is entitled to his sweaty palms and nervous twitches before a big race, then certainly the huskies, too, can be expected to exhibit the same type of excitement. The noise of nearby barking dogs alone might drive a team into a frenzy even before it's harnessed. Even the noise of thousands of humans will do it. Put those sounds together and combine them with the innate thrill of the anticipation of running, and it often takes a dozen or more people to tie a sled dog team into the tug lines and hold it steady for the crucial minutes before the start of the Fur Rendezvous.

Volunteers help each musher keep the dogs in place so that they don't haul the sled across the starting line before the musher's turn. Once the dog is lifted out of his box on the back of the truck, he is eager to run; starter's commands are irrelevant. Eyes bulging, muscles tensing, barking madly, the dog strains at his harness. One by one the dogs are led to the sled this way, and all are eager to go.

The scene is a madhouse as teams are hooked up and inched to the starting line. Usually, there is a handler who calms each dog while the musher stands on the back of the sled, his weight the only other thing holding the hungry dogs back.

On the afternoon of the first heat of his first Rendezvous, Attla remained focused on his dogs. Some of them, after all, had been in Fairbanks for the North American and raced in front of big crowds. Those dogs were as level-headed as any dogs could be, and it was up to them to lead their inexperienced teammates through the race. George's job was to keep the lines of communication open so they would remember all they'd been taught. He, too, had to concentrate.

Sprint mushing races begin with staggered starts, and the starting order is determined by a blind draw. A mass start would produce an unnecessary tangle that could jeopardize musher and dog safety, so even the smallest races start with some interval between mushers. The time differential is ironed out at the end of the race, so the first dog team back to the finish line isn't automatically the winner. It takes some math to figure out who wins.

It was warm out, and the trail was smooth for the first heat. On that afternoon, the world of sprint mushing changed forever. It took only one heat, twenty-five miles of racing, for George Attla to thrust himself into racing prominence and public consciousness.

"Three, two, one. Go!" the announcer shouted into the public address system.

And Attla's dogs went. The village team from Huslia sprinted down Fourth Avenue, turned down a side street, and raced into the nearby woods. The trail undulated over several hills, weaved in and out of thick timber, crossed more streets and small bridges over Campbell Creek, and turned once again onto Fourth Avenue for the sprint for home.

Anchorage has grown substantially since 1958. In the last thirty-five years the population has increased fivefold, to 230,000. With new homes, new strip malls, new businesses going up all the time, it has become a major city. The course was slightly different thirty-five years ago. But despite the modifications, much of the route remains the same. It was all new to Attla then, though.

Perhaps there were spectators who thought Attla's dogs were running too fast and would burn out. Perhaps there were spectators who turned to a neighbor and asked, "Who is that guy?" For the most part, though, the fans who lined the fences on the main streets and who lined the course in sparsely populated areas, did not realize what they were seeing. They cheered for everyone indiscriminately, or for personal friends and favorites in particular, or for the famous, like Wright. They could not have known just how fast Attla was going. They would find that out later.

"The dogs went fast right from the beginning," said Attla. "It went smoothly, and there were no problems."

Dogs can tire, dogs can get hurt, dogs can run off the course or tangle their lines. All of that costs time. A dog that refuses to pull, or one that gets hurt, must be loaded into the sled basket and carried back to the finish line. That's a double whammy. Not only isn't the dog working in synchronization with his pals, but he becomes dead weight for them, an additional burden to be hauled along the trail. All of those events can interrupt a race, but this time nothing went wrong for Attla.

Attla's dogs crossed under the finish banner, still pulling hard, the musher pushing hard behind them and kicking with his good leg. Sweat poured down his brow, and his wavy jet black hair was soaked and matted. Both Attla and his team had gone all out.

"I didn't know where I'd finished," he said, "but I did know that I'd gotten the best performance out of what I had."

One by one, the racers crossed the finish line. Earl Norris, a two-time champion, Lombard, making his debut in big-time Alaska racing, and Wright.

Who was the first-day leader? There was chatter among spectators, speculation that the new guy from the Bush had gone pretty fast. What was his name? Then there was a roar. The winner of the first heat was announced—George Attla.

The unknown from Huslia had walked in, racing for the first time, and taken the lead. No one could believe it. This was like some stranger from the country riding his plough horse up to the starting line at the Kentucky Derby and establishing a lead for the first few furlongs.

Fans and reporters converged on Attla. What's your background, son? How did you do it? In later years, he became the most engaging and forthcoming of athletes with the media, but in 1958 Attla was both naive and shy. Besides, this was only the first of three days of racing, so two-thirds of the competition remained. It wouldn't do to get too cocky now.

Attla's time for the first heat was one hour, fifty-seven minutes, six seconds. That meant his average speed hovered at around twelve miles per hour. Sidney Huntington was right. Attla's team was world championship caliber. Wilbur Sampson finished second in the field of twenty-five mushers, twenty-seven seconds behind. Wright came in third, two minutes, five seconds behind Attla.

"I had never even heard of Attla," said Wright. "I didn't know anything about him. I was surprised he came in and won. For him just coming in, I never expected him to win like that." He congratulated Attla. It was the beginning of both a friendship and competitive rivalry.

Even if Attla himself was anonymous, Wright soon came to realize how he built his team. Wright knew some of the mushers who lent dogs to Attla, and he guessed that, being from Huslia, Attla had access to some of the best dogs in the state.

"Once we found out where his dogs came from," said Wright, "he wasn't a mystery. Huslia was the first village where people combined their dogs."

Bobby Vent, who later finished second in the first Iditarod race and who placed second in the 1956 Fur Rendezvous, said pooling the dogs was the way mushers like himself from Huslia could get their chance to compete. The families just couldn't afford to keep enough dogs around to build their own competitive teams and send a musher outside the village to compete.

"We knew we had good race dogs," said Vent, who is in his eighties and still lives in Huslia. "Any time anybody went out with them, they did pretty well. We all figured this was the only way we could do it. George was interested and we all felt we had to pull for him."

Two minutes is a good lead in the three-day Rondy, but it is not insurmountable. Remember all those things that can go wrong? Such a lead can evaporate swiftly. A musher must recognize the signs of fatigue in the dogs and realize which ones he might be better off benching for the second and third days. And even so, he can expect his second day heat to be slower than the previous day's. Often, it is the dog team that slows down the least over the second and third days of the Rendezvous that emerges with the victory. So building a lead was exciting for Attla, but it did not make him champion.

Attla allowed himself to enjoy his moment, to revel in the day's victory for a while, but his concentration held firm, and he did not lose his focus on the race. This was especially valuable because not long after the heat ended and the dogs were watered, fed, and bedded down for the night, George faced a problem.

A smart musher takes readings from his dogs, but a smart musher also reads his own body. On the night of his first victorious heat in the Rendezvous, Attla's entire body ached from the exertion. All his muscles were stiff and sore. He had been running on adrenaline and, by going out so hard, he had exhausted himself.

"I didn't know my own physical strength," he said. "I didn't know how to pace myself. In all my training, it had never entered my mind that I would get that tired. I had given everything I had, and the next morning I couldn't move."

He was no longer anonymous George Attla. He was now leading the world championship race. He had become famous overnight in the newspapers and he knew that all over the state Alaskans were listening to his exploits. Now everyone knew his name, and the worst of all possible scenarios unfurled in his mind. It would be possible, if he did not renew his strength, that he could plummet out of sight just as easily as he rocketed to the top.

Attla tried to block out his situation, tried to think only of winning. He spent the night at the home of his friend, Clyde Bastian, who was also racing. They stayed up late talking about the race, the crowds, and his chances. Bastian encouraged him, told him he could do it. That kept Attla's head in the game. But he still had to drag himself to the starting line. His body was so sore from the first day, it affected his race. He, not his tired dogs, was the biggest liability. As the first day leader, Attla was the first one out of the starting chute for the second day of the 1958 Rondy.

There was a major realignment of the standings that day. Wright won the second day's heat in two hours, three minutes, thirteen seconds. Attla's sharpness improved as the race went on, and the dogs performed admirably. Attla's heat time was just two seconds slower than Wright's that day, which preserved his overall lead.

"I was okay once I got limbered up," said Attla. "I got better, but I'll tell you, it was many years before I really learned how to pace myself."

Attla once again spent a quiet night at the home of Bastian, who dropped out after the second heat, and this time the rest revived Attla. The initial shock to his body had worn off, and he felt fine for the rest of the race. The crisis was over.

On day three, Attla whipped the field, turning in a time of two hours, two minutes, fifty-seven seconds. He completed the race with nine of the eleven dogs he started with. Sampson rallied and Wright fell off, and although Wright finished second overall in elapsed time, Attla's winning time of six hours, three minutes, eighteen seconds for the seventy-five miles won the race by close to three-and-a-half minutes.

This time, when his dogs trotted across the finish line, Attla knew immediately that he won the championship. The crowd stomped and hooted, clapped, and shouted his name. "Attla! Attla!" It felt unreal.

Attla had never known such a rush of happiness. Despite what surely must have been ridiculous odds, his dream had come true.

"I'm the best in the world," he thought as he basked in the applause on Fourth Avenue. "I'm the best."

"I was the world's championship dog musher. That's what I had wanted to do, and that's what I did. And there were a lot of people there to see it. I can hardly describe the way it felt."

One thing was stunningly clear, however. George Attla had found his place. The young man with the stiff leg had proven himself to his family, his friends, his neighbors, indeed, to the whole world.

"That one trip," said Attla, "was one of the most important things in my life. It just kind of set up my life for me."

The triumph in the 1958 Fur Rendezvous World Championship set up one of the most amazing careers in all of sports. No one, not Attla, nor any of the many fans that February day, could have imagined that they witnessed the beginning of something that would last so long. Thirty-five years later, George Attla is still racing, and the children of those spectators' children will be watching him contend for more sprint mushing championships.

Chapter 10

Dog Man

Rose Ambrose and her family were beaver trapping on the Yukon River during the 1958 Fur Rendezvous. Their next-door neighbors had a radio that picked up a Fairbanks station, and on the show "Tundra Topics" it was announced that the new world champion dog musher was George Attla from Huslia. "I was so happy," said Attla's sister. "I was surprised. I didn't know what to think before the race. I thought there were all these white guys out there with their expert dogs. And to be out there in Anchorage and to win, I thought, 'Did it really happen?'"

The Attla family was spread all over the region at trapping camps, awaiting word on George's race. Some could hear the news on their own radios, others had to wait to be given the information. Rose said that later her mother, Eliza, told her she fell asleep and her father, George, Sr., burst into the bedroom when he heard of George's victory.

"Daddy just woke her up, shaking her and yelling, 'George won! George won!' She said, 'Huh? Huh?' She was in a deep sleep. She was sleeping so hard, she was in shock when she woke up and heard that. It was a great day." A great day for all of the Attlas. Steven, whose dogs played an important role in the race and whose encouragement helped George get to the starting line, was also at a trapping cabin. He was alone with his own radio and couldn't believe his ears when news of his brother came through. "Oh, it surprised me when he won," said Steven. "Listening to that race, by golly, I was proud of him."

Robert Attla was also trapping, but he rearranged his day to start extra early so he could be home in time to listen to the radio. "We knew his chances were good," said Robert. "We could recognize a championship team in the village. Those three days, though, that was the biggest excitement we had for a long time."

George Attla was the toast of the town in Anchorage, too. Perhaps Gareth Wright understood how Attla had combined top dogs from top mushers to win, but to most people Attla was a thousand-to-one shot coming in, a lightning bolt striking. They couldn't believe it.

The common reaction was, "Where have you been keeping yourself? How come we never heard of you?"

"I was treated really well," said Attla. "The funny thing was I was still inexperienced. A lot of the mushers played mind games during the race trying to psyche each other out, but nobody played those with me because nobody knew me."

That was the last time that would ever happen, and, in fact, later in his career, Attla would become known as the king of psyche himself, like all those football coaches who lower expectations until the alumni think the team can't even beat Ding Dong School.

Overshadowed in the excitement of Attla's startling victory was the Fur Rondy debut of Dr. Roland Lombard, the slightly built veterinarian from Wayland, Massachusetts. Lombard finished fourth in his inaugural Rondy, also an impressive showing for a rookie—even if another rookie had garnered most of the attention.

Lombard, who died in October 1990 at the age of seventy-eight, made his mark on Alaska sprint dog racing simultaneously with Attla. While Attla had more outdoors savvy and practical experience from growing up in the wilderness, Lombard brought scientific knowledge and training methods to the sport.

At first, Alaskans look down on interlopers. They are skeptics who doubt whether outsiders understand them and their ways.

Visitors must record a significant achievement before they are accepted. Alaskans do not give their hearts or respect to the outsiders who come to town and are quickly driven off by the challenges of the land and weather. But once a man shows he is in it for the long haul—even in the case of Lombard who never moved to Alaska but spent several months a year in the state—they adopt him. Lombard was indeed embraced as a favorite and, during his racing years, accorded a respect that matched Attla's.

There were several reasons for that. On the basis of accomplishment alone, Lombard could not be denied his due. He won eight world championships in Anchorage. Secondly, his personality endeared him to everyone. He was soft-spoken and friendly and gave advice freely.

"Dr. Lombard was about as close to a true gentleman as you find," said Jim Welch. "It's hard to find anyone who didn't like him. He was a fierce competitor, and I think George respected him a great deal."

Attla did respect Lombard a great deal. When Lombard died, Attla said, "He was about the best there was. He taught me a lot."

They were gracious words for a departed rival who had suffered from a long illness before his death. The rivalry between Attla and Lombard was always an intense one, even if it was also a cordial one. The two men sought to beat each other's brains out on the race course as surely as Muhammad Ali and Joe Frazier did in their heavyweight boxing matches. But then they drank a beer with each other when the racing was all over. The two champions even trained together at times.

Attla noticed that Lombard had Siberian huskies, which the Alaskans didn't think much of (though that view changed in later years), and he thought it was amazing that a guy from the East Coast could finish fourth.

"We had had mushers come to Alaska before from the lower forty-eight, and they all brought up the rear," said Attla. "I remember a lot of people being real happy about him doing well, because we felt his finishing that high would encourage more mushers to come up. They didn't know how good he was going to be. The others had come to Alaska, got clobbered, and never came back. But he was competitive right away."

Attla said Lombard was so quiet he could sit in the same room and you would never know he was there. Not so Gareth Wright, the three-time champion.

"Gareth was a presence," said Attla. "He'd tell you he was a threat to you. Gareth always had a smile on his face, but he was confident and very vocal. If he thought he was going to beat you, he said so."

Attla, Lombard, and Wright would be the three chief contenders for the big titles in the sprint mushing world for some time, and they were three very different people. Attla catalogued his first impressions of the two men without, of course, knowing that they would be closely linked for years to come.

"I had no idea then," said Attla, "but all my career those two guys were the biggest threats to what I was doing, for fifteen years. Lombard and I got most of the wins, but Gareth was always there, always a threat." Wright is the only musher whose longevity rivals Attla's, and he won the North American championship in 1950 and 1983, thirty-three years apart. Future researchers reviewing the lists of winners will likely think that it was two different people, that one was a junior.

"Gareth did some fantastic things with dogs," said Attla.

Attla and Lombard had minimal contact before and during the 1958 race, but after it was over, Lombard, still very much in the process of building a team, approached Attla and wanted to buy his leader, Tennessee.

The offer surprised George. In the Fifties, it was common practice to share dogs among friends, to perhaps trade them, if there was a good reason, or to give them away. Nobody bought dogs from a stranger. It just wasn't done.

"We only gave them away, like my brother Steven had done,"

said Attla. "I only owned two dogs on my winning team, and one of them was Tennessee. I think Steven gave me the other one, too. I told Lombard the dog wasn't for sale, and that it had been given to me."

Lombard kept pushing Attla, though, because he really wanted the dog. Lombard didn't live in an area where dogs easily changed hands, but Attla felt it wasn't proper to sell the dog—even though he wasn't especially attached to the animal. Then he decided the appropriate thing, if Lombard wanted it so badly, was to make a trade.

At that time, mushers used iron runners on wet days. Attla said he'd give Lombard the dog for a pair of runners. The bargain was made.

Compared with today's dog trading, this was a lopsided swap, with Lombard getting the better end of the deal. Selling dogs was unheard of then, although it's common now and is one way Attla has maintained a large lot of dogs over the years. Lombard took Tennessee back to Massachusetts, though he never raced him in Anchorage against Attla. It wasn't until 1963 that Lombard became a world champion. That dog was one of the many that helped him develop his team.

Attla was much more concerned with the immediate future. His prize money of fifteen hundred dollars was needed just to get him back home through Fairbanks once more. Before he left Anchorage, though, he bought a case of vodka for a big celebration party in Huslia.

"I was really looking forward to getting home," said Attla. "I couldn't wait to see what the reaction would be that I could really do it."

He left Anchorage with the idea that he would be back the next year to defend his title. He thought about it all the way home.

The whole village greeted Attla when he arrived back in town, and all its residents trooped over to his house for the party. There was much handshaking, backslapping, whooping, and hollering from relatives, friends, and even neighbors who never imagined George had it in him.

No one had a better time than Attla, who had come so far. "I'm happy for you," people said over and over. "We're so happy for you."

For the longest time, Sidney Huntington watched from a distance as Attla soaked up congratulations, then he took Attla aside and reminded him of what he'd told him long before George ever journeyed to Anchorage. "I knew you could do it," said Huntington. "I told you, you could do it."

It was a moment that stuck with Attla, a moment he appreciated, because Huntington was one of the few who had said it long before the reality. Now, when Huntington explained to Attla why he believed so strongly in him, Attla could smile back with confidence.

"Some people are natural-born dog men," said Huntington. "And some people spend lots of money and don't get anywhere. You could tell right away George was a dog man just from the way the dogs responded to him. He had the determination and the natural affinity for the dogs."

And not everyone can build and train his own dog team, either. Attla had proven he could race and beat the best. He was giddy from his accomplishment, basking in his success. But, standing in the comer at the party, watching from a different view, was Bobby Vent.

George had just shown that he was the best dog musher in the world, right? Wasn't that enough? It was enough for most people. Yet Vent was able to break through Attla's celebratory mood with one prodding comment.

"We were partying," said Attla, "drinking this case of vodka I brought home, and as we were sitting around, he said, 'You didn't prove nothin' to me.'"

That was a conversation stopper. Attla looked up at Vent. Others stopped talking.

"He said, 'All those dogs were trained by someone else before you got them. So in my eyes, you haven't proven to me that you're a dog man.'"

Vent was older and to be respected. Even if Vent's timing could have been better, he made a telling point. If the simple, ultimate compliment for a man like George was to tell him he was a true dog man, then he hadn't quite earned his spurs. Being a good dog man implied doing much more than winning one race, even if it was the biggest of all races. To Vent, a good dog man raised his own dogs, trained his own dogs, raced his own dogs, and won with his own dogs.

"That was a real dog man," said Attla.

More than three decades later, with all that Attla has accomplished in sprint mushing, Vent said he did not remember making the remark. But Attla never forgot the comment. He viewed it less as an insult than as a motivator. He never actually told Vent that he was going to show him he was a real dog man, but the determination took hold. "I thought, 'I'm going to prove to you that I'm the best dog musher there is.'"

Attla was the reigning world champion, though. His win had vindicated his belief that he found the proper direction for his life. He had performed the remarkable feat of making the Rendezvous his first win. It was the stuff of make-believe, Hollywood stuff.

"I had convinced myself that, yes, this is what I am," said Attla, "this is what I want to do. This is the thing. But when Bobby Vent told me that, it really made me want to be the best. I decided that I was not gonna go back to race just to be a racer. I was going back to win the race.

"I think if Bobby Vent hadn't said what he said, I would've probably come back the next year to Anchorage and got whipped real bad with some thrown-together team," said Attla. "That's what I think because there's no way I could have gotten the same dogs back. They were all owned by different people and I had sold Tennessee to Doc Lombard." Attla pledged to himself that he would not compete in the Anchorage Fur Rendezvous again until he could race with dogs he had trained and developed himself.

Four years passed before Attla returned to the world championship.

Chapter 11

Tough Winter

George Attla almost never got a chance to defend his Fur Rendezvous crown at all. In 1959, a year after he won the championship, he almost died.

George went back to trapping to make a living during the winter following his victory. Shirley, who had become George's first wife the year after she left Hughes, went to Huslia with him to set up a trapping camp.

Early in the season, at the end of September, before freeze-up, they traveled by boat to their territory some fifteen miles from Huslia to set the traps for the winter. It was just about the time of the first snowfall, and they hoped enough snow would fall so they could mush the dog team back to the village.

Attla intended to build a new sled, so he set off into the forest with an ax to chop down a birch tree. He found the tree that he thought would do the job and started whacking away with the ax, building up a sweat, feeling the muscles in his arms tighten and relax.

Suddenly, on one swing of the ax, the handle slipped, and instead of hitting the tree just right, the blade shifted and slashed his left foot. It was a terrible cut, but he managed to walk and hop back to the cabin. Shirley was there and grew alarmed when she examined his bleeding foot. Far from trained help, they did their best and sewed the cut closed, but that was not the end of the problem.

"I guess we didn't do a very clean job of it," he said. "It got infected and I got blood poisoning."

Blood poisoning is dangerous even if a hospital is nearby, but in the woods, far from help, it can easily be fatal. The climate, too, conspired to hold the Attlas as prisoners in their camp. The water was freezing, so they couldn't negotiate back the way they'd come by boat, yet the ice wasn't thick enough to walk on or mush over. They couldn't cross lakes or rivers.

Attla ran high fevers, and his foot throbbed. He had trouble thinking clearly, but one thought surfaced repeatedly: if he didn't get out of the camp and find medical assistance, he could die. George had heard many Athabascan Indian legends about medicine as he grew up, but he was not a true believer. He heard talk of how locks of hair held up and prayed over could possibly cure illnesses, or how feeding certain birds might produce good luck. These spiritual connections were not grounded in the harshness of everyday life, but involved beliefs in the mystical and tribal legend.

However, one night a few days after suffering the injury, in the midst of a fitful sleep, Attla was awakened by a peculiar noise. He thought he might be hallucinating, but Shirley heard it, too. Attla remembers being scared at first, then decided it sounded like someone else snoring right next to his feet.

Immediately after the noise subsided, so did the swelling. The lymph nodes in his arms and legs began shrinking back to normal. The poison apparently had run its course, had dissipated without medical care, and the fever had broken. Attla has no explanation for that except to believe that some spiritual medicine interceded.

As he began to feel better, Attla was able to think more clearly. The air temperature had been dropping. It was very cold now and he wondered whether the ice would be thick enough to support their weight if they tried to make a river or lake crossing.

"Maybe there's enough ice to go to town now," he suggested to Shirley. But he didn't have the strength to stand on the runners of an old sled for the ride, so he climbed in the sled basket and let Shirley mush.

The first creek they came to was frozen, and the dogs eagerly rushed down the steep embankment out onto the ice. But the early-season freeze-up can be tricky and misleading. This was only a thin layer of ice, and the sled plunged through into the frigid water.

"We were lucky the water was not very deep," said Attla. "The sled started to tip over sideways in the water and I put my hand out and hit bottom."

The dogs pulled hard, righted the sled, and pulled them across the creek. "I realized right away, though, there was no way we could make it," he said. "We had a long way to go and a lot of water to cross. So we turned around and went back to the trapping cabin."

Two weeks had passed since Attla cut his foot, and even though he felt better, he was far from healthy. His foot was improving, but it wasn't healed, and he couldn't walk.

George and Shirley stayed in the trapping camp another four days before two of Attla's brothers mushed in to find them. The ice had become more reliable, and they started to worry when the couple didn't return to the village. The men grew alarmed when they approached the camp and saw no evidence of travel or trails in the vicinity. They figured something had happened, and they were right. They rescued George and he recuperated at home; he never went to the hospital. The serious injury just healed itself in time.

The accident started a year of living dangerously for Attla. Less than a month after recovering from the blood poisoning, he stuck himself with a metal snow hook.

Mushers command their dogs to stop running, but to help them slow down they step on a brake that drags through the snow. Then, once the dogs stop, the drivers anchor the sled with a snow hook to prevent runaways. Attla was experimenting with a new metal hook with sharp points when he had his second accident.

For years, trappers had counted on their dogs to obey the order to sit still, but Jimmy Huntington had come back to the village displaying the newfangled gear, and it appeared to be a worthwhile innovation. You could stop your dogs anywhere at all and feel confident they'd stick around no matter what mood they were in. The hook worked. Attla was running eight dogs, and every time he put the hook in the snow, they didn't budge—until the time he jammed it hard into the snow, started walking up to the front of the team to straighten a harness, and the dogs jerked the hook out of the ground. It flew through the air, and the point imbedded itself in his thigh.

Attla half caught the hook as it entered his leg and deflected some of the impact. Still, the blood began flowing at an alarming rate. He used a rope as a tourniquet to stop the bleeding and mushed himself back to town. "That was a tough winter," he said.

Chapter 12

Super Dogs

In his heart, George Attla was impatient. But he forced patience on himself. It was very hard to sit by the radio five hundred miles from Anchorage and listen to the Fur Rendezvous World Championship in 1959. And again in 1960. And again in 1961.

Very hard. He ached to return with a team of fresh dogs and show the world that his win in 1958 hadn't been a fluke, that he was, indeed, the best sprint dog musher in the world. Instead, he sat at home as fans and other mushers forgot about him.

Every time he was tempted to scratch his itch he remembered the words of Bobby Vent, and his work building and training his very own team grew into a mission.

"I could have gone back," said Attla. "But I wouldn't have won. I had to be patient. I wanted to make sure that when I went back I would win. Every winter I trained dogs. My dogs were getting better."

Ironically, Attla's summer work played a crucial role in making him a success in mushing. He had a good job as a riverboat pilot on the Yukon River and made a thousand dollars a month in summers, more than enough to live on and still put some in the bank. Unemployment compensation, plus any income from trapping, tided him through the winter.

In the early Sixties, a new product was sweeping the north

country. The snowmachine had arrived, the iron dog that could go much farther and faster than a team of huskies.

The snowmachine revolutionized the thinking of the North. Athabascans and Eskimos who had for so long depended on and bonded with dogs, discarded the long relationship for the latest technological advancement. Even if the snowmachine wouldn't start in extreme cold weather, couldn't be easily fixed without replacements being flow in at high cost, didn't know the way home on its own, and had no sixth sense to warn its owner of dangerous, marginally frozen waters, Alaska Natives were excited by the snow-go and chose machine over dogs.

Freddy Vent, Bobby's son, owned a good team of nine dogs, but he was smitten with the idea of buying a snowmachine. Because of his summer earnings, Attla could afford to buy one, even though he didn't want one. He wanted good dogs. So Attla bought a snowmachine and traded it to Vent for his dogs.

One of the dogs in that bunch was Nellie, a black dog with two white dots above her eyes. Nellie became the first great leader for George Attla.

"When I first started to run her," he said, "I could tell she was an exceptional dog. And there were five others in there that you could see were champions. I had a whole yard of super dogs."

Nellie was the standout. "She had the athletic ability and was willing to please," Attla said. "A lot of heart, really. She did everything I wanted her to do—and you don't get that often."

As in any team sport, there is no special treatment for a star athlete. Coach Attla treated all his dogs equally in the dog yard, at feeding time, and on the trail. There is, after all, little room for sentiment in the sport, and racing dogs are not to be confused with pets. Nevertheless, the best dogs do find soft spots in a musher's heart. The fondness grows, Attla said, when the musher learns he can count on a leader—a leader like Nellie. She came through every time, and he couldn't help but respect her talent and be grateful for her leadership abilities.

"I treated them all the same," he said, "but I was proud of certain dogs. They made the difference between winning and losing."

Once surpassed by younger, faster teammates, however, few racing dogs retire to a life of leisure. Attla eventually sold Nellie to Roland Lombard.

Attla teamed the dogs he received from Freddy Vent with the dogs he already owned and some he obtained from his father-in-law, Abraham Oldman, shaping them into a racing team of eleven quick dogs. By 1961, he had the core of a team he thought could win another world championship.

He sensed, though, that he might yet be a couple of dogs shy of having a perfect team. The one disadvantage he had compared with other village mushers was his long summer absence. While he made good money on the Yukon, he also missed out on a lot of dog trading. "The reason I had such a small team," said Attla, "was by the time I got home the dogs were already gone. They were lent out or dealt away."

Building a good team thirty years ago required good business acumen as well as good dog judgment. Attla had to locate and identify top-notch dogs and persuade the owners to part with them. He got lucky with Freddy Vent, but in the winter of 1962, just when he felt prepared to return to the Rendezvous he had some bad luck: two of his dogs came up lame one day. They couldn't race, but since they could still work, he gave them to George, Sr., for his trapline.

Two other local racers, Bergman Sam, and Cue Bifelt, who had won the 1960 world championship, were also training for the Rendezvous. They, too, were trying to round up every available dog, but there just weren't enough around the village to supply three quality teams. And Attla still needed some fill-ins. "I could see I had the fastest team, but I didn't have enough dogs. I didn't want to be outnumbered."

He was sure he had the fastest team for a short distance, or maybe for a single day, but he needed a bigger team with the staying power for a three-day race. Attla's brother-in-law, Bill William, was training a team for the North American in Hughes.

Since the North American is a full month after the Rondy, it was possible for the dogs to run both races comfortably. At the last minute, just before heading to Anchorage for the Rendezvous, Attla swung a deal with William. He told him that if he could borrow a few of his dogs, he'd lend him his whole team for the North American. William went for the deal.

Besides Nellie, there was one other notable husky in this Attla team. George came by it in a curious way. The dog's name was Tuffie, and it originally belonged to Attla's first benefactor, Sidney Huntington, a man who raised his dogs for the trapline and refused to participate in the wheeling and dealing.

"The dogs are for trapping and that's what I'm going to use them for," he would announce, "not racing."

At the time, it was rare for the men of Huslia to party. Alcohol was scarce in the Bush, so it was only on the special occasions when hard liquor was available that some serious partying took place. About six months before the 1962 Rondy, Attla was drinking heavily with his brother Frank, Huntington, and his brother-in-law, Georgie.

The party got wilder and wilder, though that was part of Attla's strategy. He wanted everyone in a good mood. He thought he might be able to talk some of the others into parting with dogs they might not consider selling when they were sober. There was raucous debate about running dogs, who had the best dogs, and who the contenders were for the world championship. Huntington allowed Attla to harness some of his dogs up with his own team for a run. "I saw immediately that one of his leaders was an exceptional animal. When we came back, we kept drinking, and I ended up with his leader," said Attla.

Attla bought Tuffie for $250. He talked Georgie out of one of his dogs that day, too. He owed his slick dealing as much to his ability to drink his friends under the table as to his own perseverance and dog judgment. Huntington never talked much to Attla about how Tuffie changed hands, but years later he confessed he remembered the incident well and now could laugh about it.

Getting Huntington's dog was one of the best deals Attla ever made; Tuffie and Nellie became an unbeatable duo. They were tough, fast, and smart, with the common sense any good leader needs. "They were a super pair of leaders," said Attla. "They had never been trained to race, though, and I trained those dogs myself."

On his way south for the Rendezvous, Attla once again stopped in Fairbanks for training with a friend who had a kennel near downtown. He brought sixteen dogs with him. Racers today have been known to start the Rondy with teams of more than twenty dogs, but at the time sixteen dogs was a very large team.

One day, on a training run, a dog chewed through the tug line and eight dogs burst free. Half the team was on the loose. Attla was mushing back toward town on the flat land on the outskirts of Fairbanks, but the dogs who escaped dashed off in the opposite direction. They did not return to the kennel on their own, as Attla hoped. After all those years of preparing, Attla's dreams were jeopardized. Just as the truck breakdown in 1958 could have ruined his first Rondy, Attla was in danger of being eliminated from contention in his second Rondy without ever getting to Anchorage.

Many things can happen to dogs when they are running through the countryside on their own. They can get lost or injured. So close to town, they could also get hit by a car. George was frantic.

Attla and his friend called around town and discovered the dogs were in the pound. So they were safe, but Attla had to bail them out, and he didn't have any money. This was another trip to Anchorage on the cheap, where every penny was counted and budgeted. His friend operated a major business in town, though, and he telephoned the chief of police to explain the situation. He was able to talk him into arranging for the dogs' freedom for free.

"Close call," said Attla.

One of the late acquisitions from Bill William was a third top leader that Attla shrewdly kept quiet about. When he got to Anchorage, Sam and Bifelt thought Attla would only be racing dogs that they'd seen in Huslia.

"They didn't think I had the dogs to carry through for three days," said Attla. "But I had a lot of confidence in those dogs. I could do anything I wanted with that team. They were really tremendous."

It had been four years since Attla raced in Anchorage. Basketball, baseball, football, dog mushing, it doesn't matter; sports are very much a what-have-you-done-for-me-lately world. There had been different champions each year: Jimmy Malemute in 1959, Bifelt in 1960, and Leo Kriska in 1961. It seemed the newspapers hardly remembered Attla. He was just one of those other one-time winners. By 1962, George had been away long enough to make any expert doubt his ability to contend once again. Everyone knew he must have new dogs, too, so Attla was in a situation where he had to prove himself again.

The fans, though, were friendly. They remembered the electrifying race Attla produced in 1958. This time, when he was introduced at the starting line, he was introduced as a past champion. That carried weight with observers—once a world champion, always a world champion. It is one of those titles, like judge, governor, or senator, that follow a man forever.

Attla, at age twenty-eight, was more mature, too. He wasn't nervous because he knew what to expect. He was quietly sure of himself because he, and only he, realized the capabilities of his dogs. Even the villagers who knew him best didn't know how good a team he had.

The trail was very fast for the Rendezvous that year with firm snowpack. His dogs sped through the first twenty-five-mile heat in one hour, thirty-three minutes, forty-six seconds. Attla was back and the fans roared. The result stunned the competition. George's winning heat time was close to four minutes faster than second-place Bergman Sam.

The reception engulfed him, and one after another, spectators shook George Attla's hand. It was like a receiving line at a wedding; the congratulations just kept on coming. "It was tremendous," said Attla.

Attla felt the single day's racing, after four years of waiting, was a vindication of his judgment. It was an emphatic response to anyone who doubted his ability to come back, to anyone who had overlooked or forgotten him.

This time, Attla hadn't worn himself out, either. The long training runs for the dogs had also trained the musher. Attla now understood his physical limitations and had learned to compensate without going overboard.

"You ache a lot in a race anyway," said Attla. "Even my arms start aching. You're bouncing around quite a bit as you go over the trail, and you've got to hold on to the sled. You have to have balance, and I use my arms more than other mushers because of the way my leg is."

A musher uses his whole body to lean into a turn, but Attla used more of his arms and shoulders to keep the sled on track. His strength was in his upper body.

On this second time around, no mistakes were made by the still-young but definitely wiser Attla.

Day two was more of the same. Attla's dogs were a minute-and-a-half faster than anyone else's. Close behind was Roland Lombard. After his own auspicious Rendezvous debut in 1958, Lombard had not emerged as a sure winner, either. In 1961, the year before, he had finished second by fifty-five seconds after a horrendous first-day heat that left him five minutes behind the leader.

In a surprising departure from form, in the 1962 race, Lombard's dogs got faster by the day, until he won the third heat. It is very unusual when a dog team does not slow a few minutes per heat. Imagine a human runner who ran five-thousand meter heats for three days in a row and got faster, not slower, with each. That performance may have been a herald of things to come in future races, but this time it was still only good enough for third place overall. Attla's dogs turned in the second fastest time in the last heat, and his winning time of four hours, forty-nine minutes, twenty seconds, gave him a six-minute margin over Sam.

"I got a big kick out of it because Bergman was surprised when he saw the size of my team," said Attla. "He thought I only had eleven dogs. After the race, he came over and saw whose dogs I had. He was so mad."

The dogs had a certain chemistry, and they responded particularly well to Attla. A month later, the same team finished third in the North American running for William; it was a good performance, but not a perfect one. Bill William, said Attla, was a brilliant dog trainer, but not always a brilliant musher.

"Not everybody can race," said George. "No matter how good your dogs are, you have to know how much fuel to burn in a given period of time. Not everybody can judge that. Bill was one of the best dog trainers I ever ran into, but in my opinion, he was not a racer."

Attla was. After collecting his prize money, he repeated his big-city purchase of 1958. He bought another case of vodka for the victory party back in Huslia. And a big communal party it was, celebrating not only Attla's win, but Sam's second-place finish and Bifelt's fifth-place finish.

Different villagers had backed different racers, but the whole village turned out for the party. And in the midst of that party, so similar to the one four years before, Bobby Vent walked up to Attla and said, "By God, you are a dog man !"

A lot of time had passed, but Vent remembered his initial words well. He was happy that he'd issued the challenge, though he really didn't expect it to have such a profound effect on Attla.

"He was a real dog man," said Vent. "A good musher who knew how to train. I didn't think he would win again because at that time not many people did. They always seemed to play out after a year. That's just the way it was. George didn't look so tough.

I still can't figure it out. He's all sinew and muscle, I guess. He's wiry, and he never gains any weight."

On the day that Vent bestowed his blessing, Attla responded the same way he'd responded the first time—inwardly. "I just smiled at him," said George. "For years, I never answered him back. I'm sure he knew he had an impact on me then, but I didn't say so, and he didn't say anything about it."

About ten years ago, some twenty-five years after Vent had challenged Attla to become a real dog man, Attla let the older man know how important he'd been to him. The circumstances that finally provoked Attla's outward expression of gratitude were unusual. One of George's sons was supposed to be racing a team his father bought for him in the Kuskokwim 300, a middle distance race in Bethel. His son had been having problems with school and alcohol, and George hoped that participating in dog mushing might straighten him out. George loaded the dogs on the plane for him, and all they needed was their driver. Only the musher never showed up to greet the dogs in Bethel.

When Attla found out the team was sitting at the airport hundreds of miles away by itself, he was furious. Bobby Vent and Jimmy Malemute were at his home, and Attla went into a tirade, ranting about the old days and how kids had changed and didn't respect their elders. Attla said he wished his own son could find an older role model whom he respected and who could advise him just as Vent had motivated him.

"I told him what an influence he'd been on me," said Attla. "Just that one thing he'd said changed my life a lot. So I told him about it then." Vent just laughed. He was surprised to hear Attla's words, but pleased.

Chapter 13

Competition

After 1962, George Attla had won two world championships; Roland Lombard had yet to taste victory. But in 1963, Doc Lombard won his first Fur Rendezvous by nine minutes over runner-up Bergman Sam. Attla finished third.

Lombard won the title again in 1964, this time edging out Keith Bryar by only fifty-nine seconds. Attla was seventh.

And once again, in 1965, Lombard captured the crown, besting Gareth Wright by two minutes, four seconds. Attla finished in fifth place. The guy from Outside could race.

"You bet we were all surprised," said Bobby Vent. "Everybody was talking about him. To come up here and beat all of us Alaska guys."

There was a new boss in town, and he wasn't even from Alaska. Lombard, who never even raced in the Fur Rondy until he was forty-five years old, was suddenly the dominant racer. Attla won two titles in four years, but Lombard won three straight. He was the target.

"I didn't think in advance that he would be the competition," said Attla. "I didn't feel threatened. It was a surprise that he could dominate. It had never happened before like that."

Although everyone wanted to beat Lombard, there was no resentment about his success. He had paid his dues, returning to

Alaska every year trying to learn the game, working to gain experience. He was such a polite man, and his demeanor earned him fans.

"He was a perfect gentleman," remembers Dick Mackey, who is best known for winning the 1978 Iditarod Trail Sled Dog Race by one second over Rick Swenson. "He never said an unkind word about anyone."

Gareth Wright agrees. "He was the gentleman of all gentlemen," he said. "He was also a fierce, tough competitor dedicated to one cause—winning. If he needed a dog, he paid the money to get it. He knew what he needed."

Lombard was the first to apply standards of veterinary medicine to dog mushing. He studied and experimented with patterns of rest and nutrition. But once he figured out a better way to do something, he shared the knowledge. "He never had a secret about his dogs," said Mackey. "He delighted in competition. He was a true leader in dog mushing."

Lombard had one other advantage over the other mushers in the early Sixties: he had more money than they did. He seemed able to afford to buy just about any dog he wanted. Most mushers lived hardscrabble existences. Lombard seemed like a multinational corporation by comparison, with many more resources.

"I didn't like him as a competitor at first," said Wright, "because he was rich and I was poor, and I thought it was his money beating me. But you couldn't fault him as a racer. And if you wanted information on how he fed his dogs, he didn't BS you. If you were smart enough to listen, you'd get better. He always helped." And at times, explained Wright, Lombard offered free vet care if a dog was sick or injured.

Attla said it took a few years to realize how Lombard was beating him. "I had to work in the summer and make money," said George. "Plus, fifty percent of my income back then was trapping. You couldn't trap and race dogs and do well. I tried to do both, but I realized it couldn't be done. In the beginning, we used to start training for the races in January, just six weeks before the

Rendezvous. It wasn't enough time. The dogs needed more time. I realized you had to train them all winter."

As the races became more competitive and mushers looked for every edge, it became apparent that the dogs needed more stamina and more speed to succeed. Lombard clued into this before other mushers, and took advantage of making money from his vet practice at other times the year.

As the sport evolved, Lombard and Attla spent enormous amounts of time trying to outsmart one another, and what evolved, along with faster dogs, was a rivalry for the ages. Starting in 1962, Lombard or Attla won fifteen world championships in the next eighteen years.

"They made dog racing what it is today," said Sidney Huntington.

Lombard was an unlikely champion; he came to the sport so late. He had dabbled in mushing at home and saved money for one trip to Alaska in 1958. He never anticipated doing well in his first race, making so many friends, or becoming so enamored of the sport.

The first time Lombard hooked up a dog sled in Alaska, under the tutelage of Anchorage musher Orville Lake, he got lost and cracked up the sled. The second time, under the direction of Earl Norris, the two-time Rondy champ, he shuddered as the sled barely missed smashing into trees as he whizzed past.

Lombard's interest in mushing stemmed from his teenage years in Maine, when he lived down the street from Leonhard Seppala, who gained fame after mushing across Alaska in 1925 to deliver diphtheria serum to epidemic-stricken Nome. He encouraged Lombard and gave him some dogs. Seppala was an Alaskan hero, as well, and inspired the creation of the Iditarod.

Still, it took Lombard thirty years to progress from hobbyist to champion racer. Once he did, though, the Fur Rendezvous was a two-man race—between Attla and Lombard.

Money aside, Gareth Wright knew Lombard had mushing ability. You could buy dogs, but you had to be smart enough to blend them, train them, and race them. It took success at all three aspects of mushing to become a complete dog man, just as Bobby Vent had reminded Attla some years before.

"When you're considered a top dog man, you know a dog inside out," said Wright. "You know its limits and its proper placement in the team. It's like being an orchestra conductor. Without a good conductor, all those instruments sound like hell."

Lombard had a bigger bankroll, but Attla had a few advantages, too. Wayland, Massachusetts, is a western suburb of Boston about twenty miles from the core of the city. Snowfall was irregular compared with the Alaska Interior. George could count on better training conditions earlier in the season, if he could take the time from his trapping to take advantage of them. That's why Lombard eventually made it a habit to move his training operation to Alaska for a month or two before the Rendezvous. Much of the time back home, he had to rely on the use of a cart instead of a sled and run his dogs over dirt trails.

Often, over the years, Attla and Lombard spent training time together. When Lombard came to Alaska for his annual visits, he stayed at Orville Lake's home in Anchorage. One of the early-season sprint mushing races that led up to the Rendezvous is now named for Lake, who was a prominent musher in the Fifties.

Attla used to go to Lake's house, and he and Lombard stayed up all night talking dogs, telling stories, and tipping a glass. The topic was always dogs, not hunting, fishing, or any other pursuit. It didn't matter who had won the race that year, the two men never took it personally.

"We respect each other to start with," Lombard told an *Anchorage Daily News* reporter in 1982. "What differences we've ever had have been minor and blew away."

Other times, they'd meet in Tok, which was originally called Tokyo, but had its name shortened by patriots during World War II. It is between Fairbanks and Anchorage on the Alaska Highway. They'd check into the Fortymile Lodge and use it as a training base. At night, they'd eat dinner, then sit around the table drinking beer and discussing training techniques.

"I learned a lot about him," said Attla. "To my way of thinking, I always have to know who I'm competing against. I have to know the person, not just the musher. We were complete opposites, but to beat a person, I have to know him as a competitor. The better I know him, his makeup, the way he thinks, the better chance I have at beating him. Of course, he learned a lot about me, too, but I never think about that. I had a lot of respect for him. There was a lot of professional respect between us."

George had easier access to better dogs than Lombard. If Lombard wanted to purchase new dogs and get to know them before the racing season, he essentially had to make a move immediately at the end of the preceding season. He could always attempt to add dogs at the last minute, but it was much better to get to know a new dog over time. Lombard had the benefit of scientific training that he applied to his animals. In 1963, Attla was surprised by Lombard's strength, but admits the superior dog team won the race.

"I was just outrun," he said. "That's all there was to it."

Sorely in need of cash, Attla sold off most of his best dogs, including the fabled leader Tuffie, and it took him years to piece together a winning team again. The time when Lombard was dominating and Attla was short of top-notch dogs was an uncomfortable period for George.

"It was really starting all over again for me," said Attla. "I went to the races, but I knew I couldn't win. The quality of the dogs was just not there. I still liked to be in the races, though. But it didn't pay. I was making a few dollars, just enough to hang on to my dogs. My pay as a riverboat pilot was better in the summertime.

"It was frustrating. I knew what I needed, but I didn't have it. I didn't have the money to buy better dogs, or enough dogs."

Being in sprint mushing for the long haul means there will always be down periods. It is a cyclical sport, and you hope that you will one day have the best dogs and be able to use them well.

"It took me a long time to build the team from 1963 on," George said, "but I never, ever sold my dogs again. I had confidence in what I was doing. I knew where I wanted to go and what I wanted to do. I just had to have patience."

As a younger man, Attla was quick to anger. He was impatient, in a hurry to get things done, get things over with—and his temper showed. But not with dogs. Dogs brought out the serenity in him. The process of turning a fair dog team into a good one cannot be rushed. "To be a good trainer, you can't show your impatience," he explained. "I kept a perfect record. I've never been able to explain that, because I'm not tolerant of people. I think it's maybe because people should know better."

By 1967, Attla thought he had a pretty good dog team again. He finished sixth in the world championships that year as Lombard won his fourth crown after an off year in 1966.

In 1968, Attla figured he was ready to show everyone that he was again the best dog musher in the world.

Chapter 14

Rivalry

George Attla pulled even with Roland Lombard in world championship titles in 1968. The score was three to three.

Now the idea of going Lombard one better took hold of George for the first time. When all the racing was done—whatever year that turned out to be—he wanted people to look back and say, "That George Attla, he was the best who ever lived." To gain that kind of respect, Attla knew, he had to win more often than Lombard did.

"I started out wanting to win the race," said George. "That's where I started in 1958. One time. But somewhere along the way my thoughts starting running along the lines of winning more races than anyone else. By 1968, I wanted to win the race, but I was also conscious of equaling Lombard's total. I think I would have felt that way no matter who had the most, but it was Lombard who had the most. It started to take shape in my mind that when I quit, I wanted to have more wins than anyone else."

It was a natural evolution of thought for a man whose desire became as renowned as his accomplishments. Some champions are easily sated, particularly in the sports realm, it seems, where repeating as title-holder is tougher than winning the first time. There is a psychological letup when a hard-fought goal has been realized. The toughness in competition, though, is as much a state of mind as it is a sense of physical readiness.

On the first day of the Rendezvous in 1968, Lombard set the pace. He established a lead of about one and a half minutes over Attla. But on the second day, over a slow trail on a warm afternoon, he ran into problems and lost more than five minutes to Attla.

The challenge for the title this time came not from Lombard, but from Bill Sturdevant, and there was a peculiar irony in that. Attla had long been friends with the Sturdevant family of Anchorage and often stayed at their home before the races. That was the case in 1968.

"Prior to the race, it didn't look like I was going to be a contender," said Bill Sturdevant, "and he was staying at our home, as usual."

Sturdevant was only fifteen years old when he first met Attla in 1962. He was a novice musher and was thrilled when Attla came for his visits. George gave him some dogs that became an important part of his team, and he loved conversing with Attla about life in the Bush. Sturdevant was fascinated by the subsistence culture, the fur ruffs on George's parkas, and his handmade moose skin boots. He was captivated by the dogs that Attla and other Native mushers brought into town.

"Their dogs were being used in people's daily lives," said Sturdevant. "They weren't kennel raised. The rapport between the musher and the dogs was especially close. They had total cooperation. The leaders handled so well. He was able to exchange dogs like exchanging parts in an automobile."

For other mushers, even those who sought success by imitating Attla's ways, dogs weren't interchangeable. Attla said it was his gift, that he could relate to dogs he didn't even know, that he hadn't raised. It was an instinct. "It's being able to read the way the dogs think," he explained. "I've always had that."

Sturdevant was winning junior races and Attla gave him tips on how to improve. Later, when he was in his early twenties and trying to make his mark in the open-class racing, Sturdevant even trained with George. But challenging Attla for the world championship was a scenario he had only pictured in his dreams.

"I had made a resolution when I was an idealistic child that if it ever came down to me and George in a race, I'd let him win," said Sturdevant. "It just meant so much to him to win and he was my teacher."

Not that Sturdevant ever figured it would happen. He never thought he'd be that good, and if he ever were, Attla wouldn't even be racing. But when Lombard faltered on day two of the 1968 race, the fantasy was reality. Sturdevant lay in fourth place after the opening day of racing, but pushed past Lombard and Charlie Belford, another New England racer, over the next two days. In fact, Sturdevant's final twenty-five-mile heat was the fastest over all three heats. He was right on George's back.

It was after the second day of racing, when Sturdevant emerged as a threat, that life back at the house became a little testy. Sturdevant began to realize just how important victory was to Attla.

They were in the basement discussing the day's racing, and Sturdevant said he didn't feel he'd had a very good run. Yet the run was the second-best of the day, and he trailed Attla by only twenty-seven seconds. Perhaps Attla thought Sturdevant was being cheeky, but when Sturdevant said that, George erupted in a rage. He picked up an object and hurled it across the room. It clattered off the wall, and he stomped away.

"I guess he didn't like hearing that he'd beaten a bad team by only a few seconds," said Sturdevant.

Sturdevant, even as a young man, was a master of psychological gamesmanship, intentional or not. It got on Attla's nerves. "He used to frustrate me," said Attla. "Oh boy, he used to frustrate me so bad in the evenings. He'd tell me, 'Oh my, the dogs ran horrible today.' Yet he was almost beating me. When he said that to me, he knew he had me mad."

On the third day, Sturdevant's team was anything but bad. "The whole idea of being first and second was out of the storybook

I had written when I was fifteen," said Sturdevant. "I was delighted."

Attla hung on to win, though, besting Sturdevant by forty-five seconds over seventy-five miles.

"For some reason, it didn't bother me that he beat me in that race," said Sturdevant. "I don't know if I'd be as idealistic now." Sturdevant never came closer to winning a world championship.

Years later, Attla insisted he was never worried that Sturdevant would beat him in the overall standings. "I could see how tough my dogs were," he said. "I had a good pair of leaders and I had a good, solid dog team. Some of the dogs Billy Sturdevant had I sold to Keith Bryar in 1963. That team went through Bryar, then Billy Solomon before Sturdevant got hold of them."

If Attla was resourceful, continually rebuilding his team, then Lombard was no less so. Clearly, ten years after he won his first world championship, Attla was still to be reckoned with and counted on as a challenger. Lombard's response? Three straight world titles.

The next three years, Lombard captured the Fur Rendezvous titles, with Attla trailing in second. This was the rivalry at its peak, with room for no one else near the front. In 1969, Lombard's winning time was five hours, one minute, fifty seconds. Attla finished just nine seconds behind. In 1970, on a mushier, slower trail, Lombard's winning time was five hours, twenty-four minutes, seven seconds, just thirty-one seconds ahead of Attla. In 1971, Lombard won by more than six minutes. The temperature hovered around the freezing mark and the trail was rough, making for much slower going. Whatever the weather conditions, the class teams—Lombard's and Attla's—led.

Victory was so tantalizingly close in 1969 and 1970, just beyond Attla's reach. His team was almost special, but not special enough to overtake Lombard. Money was always a major factor in what kind of dogs Attla brought to Anchorage. Attla needed a larger pool of dogs, but he couldn't afford them.

In addition, feeding the team grew more expensive. In the past, dogs lived on many of the same dietary staples as humans—dried salmon and the like. But as the dogs got faster and the sport of sprint mushing grew more competitive, dog food companies developed brands richer in nutrients and vitamins. A musher had to mix some processed dog food into his dogs' diets to keep up.

"The hardest part was not being able to do it financially," said Attla. "It was hard living in Huslia and trying to ship dog food up there. If you bought a bag of dog food in Fairbanks, its price was doubled by the time you got it to Huslia. The shipping costs were killing me.

"Every dog in my yard was a top race dog, but I'd only have twelve, and I'd have to go around trying to borrow or lease four more dogs every year before the Rendezvous. I didn't have any extra dogs. I had to start over every year." He couldn't afford to keep litters of puppies around the house anymore, waiting to discover whether they could cut it as racing huskies.

"I could tell fast—after two runs—if a dog was going to be a champion," said Attla.

He looked for a firm gait and a level arch of the back. If the dog didn't have the right form, he sold it to another musher. Though he relied on snap judgments, he never made a big mistake. No puppy he judged as lacking championship stuff ever became the leader of another musher's winning team.

Weeding out the puppies that he was confident couldn't carry his team to a title was one skill; identifying the dogs that would become great leaders was another.

Of the seventeen good, promising pups he once knowingly sold as a friendly gesture to a musher who needed his help, several eventually filled out a North American championship team.

Lingo, Attla's favorite dog of all time, impressed him immediately. He stood out not just because he was all white, but because he had the ability to take commands.

"Right away I knew he was going to be a fantastic leader. He looked like he was born to the position."

Another pup from the late 1980s, named Chief, seemed to have similar ability. Attla figured he had another long-term winner who could lift his team to the top. Chief moved into the first team as a two-year-old and performed well. But one day Chief appeared listless and wouldn't eat. Though clearly sick, the dog showed no signs of serious illness. Attla brought him into the house for the night and placed him in a crate to keep out the drafts. The next morning, when Attla awoke, Chief was dead.

There have been other puppies that Attla knew had the potential for greatness that became disappointments. He tried to put these dogs out of his mind as soon as possible.

"These were dogs that had the physical ability but not the heart," he said. "They think they're racing because they like to run, but some of them get too smart and they know it's not that much fun."

During the winter of 1991-1992, Attla groomed fifteen two-year-olds as future racers, but only eight made the team. One of the seven that didn't was Less, a dog with all the promise in the world. Attla figured that he didn't think it a special honor to become part of the George Attla racing team, and when the dog chose not to run in the style to which the musher had become accustomed, Attla sold him.

"It's a disappointment when that happens," he said. "You know the dog can do it, but he won't. Other mushers may want these dogs. Maybe they're not as demanding as me."

In essence, the Sixties belonged to Lombard, who won five titles before the decade ended. For almost eleven months of the year, Lombard was invisible by Alaska standings. The village mushers partied together at spring carnivals in the communities clustered around the Yukon River, and they ran into each other at fish camps in the summer. Lombard was back near Boston, tending to his veterinary practice.

But he was also tending to his dog mushing. Norman Vaughan, the oldest musher ever to finish the Iditarod (he completed the race at the age of eighty-four in 1990), was a Lombard handler in Massachusetts and Alaska.

Vaughan, who left Harvard in 1928 to go to Antarctica with Admiral Richard Byrd, has been around dogs most of his life. In the Sixties, he frequently worked with Lombard and his dogs in Wayland, spending nights in the Lombard home with Doc and his wife, Louise.

"Doc often worked twelve-hour days," Vaughan recalled.

Vaughan made two visits to Alaska with Lombard as his handler. On one of those trips, he made his own sprint mushing debut with Lombard's second-string team in a race on the Kenai Peninsula, some 150 miles from Anchorage.

Just like Attla, it seemed, Lombard was always looking to gain an edge. He was so meticulous in his preparations, that he anticipated all eventualities.

On one of his five-thousand-mile drives from Boston to Anchorage, Lombard crashed his truck. He wasn't hurt and neither were the dogs, though they were frightened at being pinned in their boxes.

"He was so concerned after that," said Vaughan, "that he made me wear a hardhat when we drove the Alaska Highway. Not like the snow-machine helmets of today, either, but a construction worker's hat.

"And he was afraid I'd lose my concentration when driving because the scenery in Alaska and the Yukon Territory was so beautiful." To guard against that, Lombard drew a thin black line down the middle of the windshield and issued orders to Vaughan: it was all right to drive and look at the scenery on the driver's half of the windshield, but if he wanted to look at the scenery on the right side of the truck, he was supposed to pull over.

That attention to detail enhanced Lombard's reputation as a man who was ready to try anything on the trail as well.

"He was always courteous on the trail," said Vaughan, "and he was generous with his knowledge about dogs. He was a pioneer in the way he watered his dogs, and I was working with him when he discovered the best way to do it. Rather than say, 'Boy, we've got something nifty, a secret weapon,' he told everybody. That's the way he was."

Yet always, Lombard was as keenly conscious of Attla as Attla was of him.

"We talked all the time about how we were going to beat Attla," said Vaughan. "We wondered what Attla was going to bring forth that year."

Although Attla later eclipsed Lombard, for a time whatever he brought forth wasn't enough. In an interview with the *Anchorage Daily News* when he was seventy and was no longer a front runner, Lombard paid Attla the same compliment Attla would return as a eulogy when the older man died. It was reported that Lombard smiled when he was asked who was the best. Acknowledging that Attla won more world championships than he did, Lombard said, "I think you could go by the numbers."

That was later, though. Back in the late Sixties and early Seventies, it looked as if Lombard might establish an insurmountable lead in compiling championships.

Losing by just nine seconds in 1969 angered Attla. Going into the race, he thought he had the best team, and coming so close to winning was irritating. After falling behind in that Rondy, Attla made a second-and third-day charge. One of the steepest portions of the Rendezvous trail is Cordova Hill, a side street in downtown Anchorage. Just two miles from the end, it is akin to Heartbreak Hill in the Boston Marathon. It is a breaker of dreams because it's hard to sprint for home uphill.

On the third day, Attla made a move and passed Lombard as they approached Cordova Hill. He was starting to pull away and was on the verge of pulling off a startling, come-from-behind win when a spectator stepped into the middle of the street to take a picture.

The dogs, exhausted from their gallant run, were distracted by the man with the camera and their discipline broke. Instead of sticking to the trail as Attla urged them to, they darted into the crowd, creating a massive tangle. Lombard took advantage of Attla's woes to pass him back. Attla got his dogs on track again and he passed Lombard once more, this time on Fourth Avenue as they neared the finish line. But he didn't beat him by enough in the final heat to make up for the earlier deficit.

Reporters got to him for reaction too soon after he finished, and he made the mistake of blowing off some steam. Usually gracious in defeat, Attla came off poorly in print this time as a woulda-shoulda-coulda man whose response to defeat sounded like sour grapes.

"My biggest problem was myself there," said Attla. "I was my own worst enemy. I'm usually okay if I get beat, if I have time to get ahold of myself. I was saying things without thinking, and when you do that you're not hurting anybody but yourself. I didn't do it again. After that I was a good loser."

But, of course, Attla didn't want to be any kind of loser. He wanted to be a winner again.

"I knew I was giving everything I had and was doing the best I could do," said George. "My personal philosophy is that when you're racing dogs and you've gotten the best possible performance you can get, it doesn't matter how you won or lost. If you got the best performance you can get, there's got to be satisfaction. He just had the superior dog team then."

There was certainly no disputing that after the 1971 Rendezvous. Lombard's margin of victory was stupendous. He was more than six minutes ahead of Attla for the seventy-five miles of racing and an unbelievable additional seven-and-a-half minutes ahead of third-place finisher young Joee Redington. If ever there was a time when the vet from the East looked uncatchable, this was it.

Attla knew he had to do something drastic to catch up. Traditional training methods and the support of his family and friends had carried him to the top level of racing. But as snowmobiles became more popular in the villages, more and more trappers relied on iron dogs rather than huskies in their subsistence lifestyle. The pool of available dogs was shrinking, since many trappers sold off their dog teams and stopped raising new ones.

By 1971, Lombard was the all-time winner in the Fur Rondy. He had five championships. Attla had won three, and he wanted to close that gap. He decided the best way to do it was to move out of the village.

"There was no way I could get all the wins I needed sitting in Huslia," said Attla.

In 1972, Attla moved from his home village to North Pole, on the outskirts of Fairbanks. Phase two of his sprint mushing career in the Fur Rendezvous World Championship was about to begin.

Chapter 15

A New Title

Not only was George Attla falling behind Lombard in the Fur Rendezvous World Championship, but he was way behind Doc in the North American Open Championships in Fairbanks, too.

The gray-haired Lombard, so much older than Attla, won his first North American in 1959. Then he won additional titles in 1962, 1963, 1964, 1966, and 1967.

By 1969, Attla, who raced the North American less frequently than he did the Rondy, had never captured the title. "It seemed like I always had too many dogs that were getting hurt, and by the time I got to the North American there were never enough dogs to be competitive," said Attla.

That's where the shortage of good dogs really hurt him. Even if he had enough dogs for the Rondy, they didn't hold up to last through both big races.

The North American closely resembles the Rendezvous both in form and in substance. Held during the third weekend in March, the North American is also a race of three lengthy heats. The first two races are twenty miles long, and the final race is thirty miles long.

In the 1969 North American, George was spurred on by two things—the manner in which he lost the Fur Rendezvous a month earlier, and concern for his father, who was critically ill.

"Back then," said Attla, "I used to race so hard I could blank everything out of my mind. Even with my dad lying there, I was so wound up I could block it out. I used to be able to complete the whole course without seeing a soul, the spectators. They were just a blur to me, a crowd of people, not individual faces. I never used to be able to see anybody that I knew. Afterwards, people would say to me, 'Did you see me? I was cheering for you on the bridge.' And I never did.

"I was good at what I did. My mind was tough. I was totally focused on what I was doing. That's a problem that I've got these days. Now I see people. It's all mental."

Like so many champions, Attla was able to muster a huge amount of adrenaline for a competition and turn his body over to it. He was so intensely wrapped up in the major competitions that he used to suffer deep depressions after the races, whether he won or lost.

"It was a physical thing," he said. "You have a terrible letdown after the race is over. I'd stay like that for three or four days until I pulled myself out of it. I was so high for the race, then I was so low when it was over. It's almost like, 'Is that all there is to it?'."

By 1969, the North American was an albatross for George. There had been other years when he felt he should have won it. He'd already proven he had top dogs by winning three world championships, but something always went wrong in Fairbanks. He was starting to doubt himself and wonder whether he could win the North American.

"I should have been doing better than I was in that race," said Attla. "Maybe I just didn't know how to win the North American, how to use the dogs right."

George, Sr., was very much on George's mind. He wanted to win the North American for his father. Even before his illness, George, Sr., had gone blind but refused to make concessions to the loss of his sight. At age sixty-eight he was a tough old man who had developed a routine and wanted to stick to it. He didn't want to vary it just because he was blind. "He still wanted to run his trapline," said Attla.

So George, Sr., ran his trapline; his dogs were so well-trained that they knew the route. Of course, George, Sr., had spent his life in the Huslia area and knew every trail. He could practically negotiate them blind anyway.

"The dogs knew where he had trapped the year before, and they would automatically stop where he had trapped," said George. "Then he would go and set a new trap. It was something he wanted to do. You couldn't keep him at home.

"My father didn't believe in sitting around, you know. He went out to fish camp, too, and one time, about three years before he died, he was at camp and was cutting wood while Mom was at home. And he knocked a tree down on himself. It was a dry tree, and not that big, but it pinned him to the ground. The main leader of the dog team, though, knew something was wrong. He chewed himself free of the harness and ran back home and got my mother. It was about two-and-a-half miles. So those dogs, they really understood the old man."

It is not so mysterious, after hearing tales like that, to see where George inherited his own dog sense.

Before the North American, Attla was aware that his father could die at any time. He was failing but trying to hold on, even if he was too weak to listen to the race on the radio. Attla gave his thoughts to his father before the race, but once it began, he thought only of the dogs. His race went smoothly the first day, but by that time his father was in a coma. His race went smoothly the second day, too, and Attla wrapped things up easily on the third. He had his first North American title.

"It was a big satisfaction," said Attla. "I thought I finally had the answer on how to run the dogs in the North American. I knew I could do it then. It seems to me, that's what it's all about. If you don't have the confidence you can do it, you can't do it."

Now Attla had done it. And he believes his father knew he

won, but he can't be certain. George, Sr., died about two hours after the race ended.

"My mom said that she thinks he knew that I won the race," said Attla. "She told him that I won. I knew he was going to go."

Chapter 16

Full-time Musher

George Attla sat in his new mobile home in North Pole. He had barely moved into a trailer court on Badger Road, just off the Richardson Highway and perhaps fifteen miles from downtown Fairbanks. He was in the house only twenty-five minutes when there was a knock on the door.

It was the police. Someone had complained about his dogs' barking. Welcome to the city. After a lifetime of living in a tiny village, where everyone had dogs and they were part of the lifestyle, Attla discovered that not everyone liked the idea of living next door to yipping huskies, whether or not they belonged to a world champion.

"That was a shock," he said. "I didn't realize people didn't want dogs around."

This was a time of transition for Attla. He split up with Shirley, his wife of sixteen years, and left his home area for a more populated section of Alaska. Briefly, they had lived in an apartment in Fairbanks near the University of Alaska-Fairbanks, but that didn't last long.

Attla, on his own, moved to the outskirts of town where he could be in the country yet still derive the benefits of being near a major population center where prices were cheaper. However, even today, the Fairbanks North Star Borough has barely sixty thousand people, so it wasn't as if Attla had moved from Huslia to New York City.

To keep the dogs quiet, Attla became a light sleeper who leaped out of bed to muzzle them any time he heard the slightest noise. This wouldn't do at all. Babies cry and dogs bark. He couldn't keep it up. He was too preoccupied with mollifying the neighbors, so he immediately began looking for a new house that was more secluded.

After a week, Attla moved out of the trailer court into the log home he still lives in. The sturdy home is just off a gravel road in a stand of towering birch trees. On sunny days, the sun climbs over the tops of the trees to splash rays of light on the kitchen and living room windows. Attla sits at his kitchen table sipping one of the dozens of cups of coffee he can drink in a day, dragging on one of the dozens of cigarettes he smokes in a day, and gazes out at his dog yard.

The individual wooden dog boxes are spaced over a cleared area reaching less than a hundred yards across to the trees, and the dogs are tied to chains that give them room to move about comfortably. On a far end of the yard are a series of pens, and here the puppies spend some of their first days after birth.

There are neighbors, but their houses are hidden by the trees, especially in summer, when the vegetation is thick, and they are neighbors who have a tolerance and appreciation for huskies.

Before he moved out of the village, Attla gained possession of more and more good dogs. The frenzy to buy snowmachines was at its peak, and he had the pick of the dogs top mushers were discarding. They were giving up the sport for a new way of life.

"I had all the best breedings to choose from up there in the Koyukuk River area," said Attla. "After all those years of people having the best dogs, people were getting completely out of dogs."

In 1970, Attla acquired a dog named Blue from Georgie Yatlin in Huslia. Then he bought some dogs from Lee Simon, another musher, including Cooley, also a first-rate dog. These dogs were aging, and they couldn't necessarily be relied on to become part of a world championship team. But they had the bloodlines, and Attla worked at breeding them before they got too old. He wanted to keep their skills alive in future generations of racing dogs.

"The breed was going to get lost," said George. "Nobody had a dog team anymore. The society was changing. I remember in earlier years, Jimmy Huntington had a pool hall in Huslia, and we used to sit around and visit there. People would come over in the evenings and the conversation would always be about dogs and who had the best team.

"But things were changing. I could sit around the pool hall and I wouldn't have anyone to talk to, because everyone would be talking about how their snowmachine was running. I had my dogs. Nobody else had dogs. It happened fast. Dogs were going out."

One other event made it easier, as well as advisable, for Attla to acquire new dogs when he moved. He obtained his first sponsor. J. C. Penney in Anchorage began paying Attla's way to the Fur Rendezvous and the North American, and his hotel expenses. It was a tremendous blessing for George, who had scraped by with borrowed money and his summer earnings.

"It meant everything," said Attla. "That was a real breakthrough. You know what that really meant? It meant that if I didn't make any money in a race, I didn't have to sell my dogs and start all over. The manager of J. C. Penney's was really interested in dogs then. They made it much easier for me."

The move to North Pole also meant that Attla was finally forsaking his trapline and his summer work as a riverboat pilot. Instead of working the river, he worked for the federal Bureau of Land Management as a line boss on forest fires. Every summer, the driest areas of Alaska's Interior are in danger from lightning fires. In a typical summer, thousands of acres burn, and there are always teams of firefighters on call to fight the blazes. For some, it is a reliable summer job.

Attla had always struggled to make a living on the trapline and his difficulties were fodder for family jokes. In the Sixties, when George went out to tend his trapline, he strapped his guitar on the sled and played it for his own amusement.

"My oldest brother Steven used to get a big kick out of me," said George. Sometimes Attla brought so much extraneous gear with him—the guitar was just one item—that he had to hook himself into his team of five or six dogs, too, in order to haul everything. Pull, George, pull.

"Everything we had back then was because we needed it," said George, "and one time I ran into him on the trail at a lake and I had the guitar. He thought that was the funniest thing."

Nothing like having a good time out there.

Attla has had nine children spaced over a thirty-year period, and while not one of them depends on trapping for his livelihood, others in the villages where he spent his youth still do.

"Most people who are running traplines out in the villages today don't have a choice," he said. "There are already too many government regulations and the country isn't big enough to support the people who are there now. None of my kids are out in the village living a subsistence lifestyle. I made sure they all moved to the city to work because I didn't think they could make a success out of subsistence living. They couldn't make a good life for themselves or their kids.

"I had happy memories living that way, but I guess you have to look at it as time moving on. That's just the way it is. But they shouldn't take away the trapping from those that still need it. That's just trying to finish off our way of life. And who's to say that someone shouldn't be able to try and live that way if they want to?"

Attla moved on right after he won his fourth world championship. The addition of so many good dogs from other village racers rejuvenated his team, and in 1972, Attla was surpassing Lombard again. After three straight runnerup finishes, he won the crown himself.

George was very proud of this team. Many of the core group of dogs he raised himself from the coupling of Blue and Cooley. That litter of pups produced fine racing dogs, including Happy, Grover, Trader, and Scottie. Another new addition to the team was a dog named Swift, purchased from Dick Mackey. Swift and Grover were two extraordinary leaders.

"George and I were good friends back then," said Mackey, who was still racing in Anchorage sprint mushing events before turning to long distance mushing. "Lombard was the man then, though. I have to believe Lombard did more for modern-day mushing in the feeding and caring of dogs than anyone else."

Lombard's mushing focus was very narrow, though. Sprinting was his game, and he wasn't that interested in middle- or long-distance events. Years later, Mackey said, he urged Lombard to race the Iditarod, the long mush across the state. "He said, 'I've never slept outdoors in my life,'" said Mackey. Attla wasn't joking when he said the two men were complete opposites.

But between 1968 and 1972, Attla made the adjustment in his own life that took the sport of sprint mushing to a new frontier, one step ahead of innovator Lombard. He began to prove that a person could become a full-time dog musher. "George is the first Alaskan who, by intent, made a living out of racing, and he still does it today," said Mackey.

"What George did," said Sidney Huntington, "was he developed an industry."

By grabbing every available good dog in the Interior, Attla became an entrepreneur. A whole vista of opportunities opened up for him in 1972. In January, several weeks before the Fur Rendezvous, he traveled outside of Alaska for the first time in his life. He was thirty-eight years old when a promoter from the Midwest, who was attempting to create a regional mushing circuit, contacted him and offered him five hundred dollars in appearance money for each race he'd enter in Michigan, Minnesota, and Wisconsin.

The first race was in Bemidji, Minnesota, and Attla got a big surprise. He'd always had the image of the lower forty-eight states as being warmer than any place in Alaska, so he left many of his heaviest winter clothes at home.

"Then I drove out, and, by God, I learned differently," said Attla. "In Minnesota, it was colder than hell. That was the biggest surprise of all. That was quite a shock to my system, I'll tell you. I wasn't dressed for it."

Attla was the only Alaskan at the three races he entered, which were generally two days of sixteen-mile heats. Lombard was there, too, as well as Charlie Belford, another Rendezvous regular, but Attla won all three of the races. He gained confidence in his team. Any team that could beat Lombard was okay. He knew that much.

As the visiting Alaskan from the place where mushing was king, George was a celebrity. Fans fussed over him, and mushers picked his brains. He was surprised by the amount of interest in the sport. At some races, there were a hundred mushers competing in the three- and five-dog classes typically reserved for beginners.

"It was completely different from racing up in Alaska," said Attla. "Everybody wanted to learn about dogs. Nobody knew anything. There were only a handful of mushers who really knew how to run dogs, but there were a lot of dogs. There were all different classes."

When the races ended, Attla was mobbed. Everyone wanted to hear his opinion on dogs. As popular as he was in Alaska, there were always divided followings among the fans. Here, Attla was the star attraction.

"The fans were more curious," said George. "They wanted to know how to do it. In Alaska, there were more people around who knew how to do it. It was a real interesting trip for me, because I couldn't talk enough to the people, they were so interested in dogs."

It was ironic: the people Attla grew up with, who had the historical links to huskies, had grown tired of dogs and were giving up on them; but in a place far removed from Alaska, he encountered overwhelming excitement and encouragement.

The year before, an enthusiastic beginner named Merv Hillpipre from Iowa telephoned Attla and bought eight dogs from him. The men met in Ely, Minnesota—a place Attla said was sort of the capital of lower forty-eight dog mushing—prior to the first race he entered. Hillpipre was a novice, but he offered to pay Attla handsomely to help make him a musher.

"He really didn't know much about dogs then," said George, "just how to exercise them and a little bit about how to get them tough."

Coming from Iowa, where growing corn was the main activity, Hillpipre's inexperience shouldn't have been too surprising. He showed Attla his collection of dogs in his truck, and George was amazed to discover he had forty dogs. Clearly, the man had serious intentions. He made a deal with Hillpipre to run his dogs, then choose which ones would make the best team. Hillpipre entered the race in Bemidji.

Hillpipre turned out to be a fast learner. The first day, Attla beat him by only fifteen seconds of running time, though it turned out to be five minutes, fifteen seconds in the standings, because Hillpipre was penalized for missing his dog team inspection in the proper starting chute.

"I just barely beat him," said George. "I hadn't realized he was that good. Eight of my dogs were in his team, though."

On the second day of racing, Hillpipre caught Attla from behind about six miles into the race and hollered, "Trail!" so that he could pass. Attla refused to budge.

"I gave him a bad time," said Attla. "There was no way he could beat me because he'd been penalized the five minutes, so I was just going along because I knew I had the race won. I told him, 'Merv, you don't need the trail. You stay back there. They'll probably penalize you another five minutes.'" Attla picked up the pace and extended his lead to the finish. It was just like putting the gas pedal to the floor in a race car.

Hillpipre was an auctioneer, and Attla said he was a nonstop talker. George found that to be an endearing trait more often than not. But, when Attla overheard Hillpipre boasting about all his mushing knowledge, he decided to give him a lesson.

"He really likes to talk and you can't shut him up," said Attla. "I was teaching him to run dogs. Then, after the race, all of a sudden, he sounded like he knew more than me, and I was his teacher. The next weekend at another race, he said, 'I want you to put my team together for me.' I said, 'No way. You're smarter than the teacher now. I'm not going to help you.'"

Attla let Hillpipre stew for a week, and he finished ninth in a race that weekend without benefit of Attla's coaching expertise. After that, Attla resumed his instruction, and Hillpipre developed into a top racer, competing in the Fur Rendezvous and the North American before he retired from mushing in 1990. In 1975 and 1978, he recorded third-place finishes in the world championships.

"I had a lot of fun with him," said George. "We became very good friends."

Fresh from his triumphant tour of the Midwest, Attla was brimming with confidence about his new dog team. This, he was sure, was an unbeatable team of super dogs.

And he was right. Nothing went wrong. No dogs dashed off in pursuit of careless fans. There were no untimely tangles. Attla overpowered the field in the 1972 Rendezvous for his fourth world championship.

The racing weather was perfect in Anchorage, with temperatures ranging from eight to twenty degrees and with superb footing on a hard, fast trail. On the first day, Attla blitzed the field by five minutes. There were no real challenges, though the rugged Gareth Wright came in second that day and held it to the end. Lombard finished fourth. Attla's astonishing winning margin was eight minutes.

Attla completed his racing season by capturing the North American for the second time.

"That was a special dog team," Attla recalled. "A superior team, much better than anyone else's. You just knew going to the track that nobody was going to beat you. They were that good. 1 think that team was way ahead of its time. They were so much better than any other dogs that were around then."

It was a team that should have been moving into its prime and been tough enough, fast enough, and experienced enough to win a few more titles. But sometimes a dynasty in the making comes undone.

Photo by Bob Hallinen

Now retired, George Attla was a contender in Alaska sprint racing championships for more than thirty-five years.

George's parents, George Attla Sr. and Eliza, pictured here about 1965, taught George the value of work.

George Attla (second from left), his first wife, Shirley, and members of his extended family get together.

Attla was only twenty-four when he won the Anchorage Fur Rendezvous World Championship for the first time in 1958.

Attla and his mother, Eliza, share a happy moment at the height of his racing career, about 1980.

Attla (left) and Charlie Champaine harness their dogs at the annual Orville Lake Memorial in Anchorage in 1990.

Attla turned down twenty-five thousand dollars for Lingo, the best dog he's ever owned.

Photo by Bob Hallinen

Attla has won the prestigious three-day North American Sled Dog Championship in Fairbanks eight times.

Attla (left) and fellow musher and friend Bill Sturdevant pause on the trail with their dog teams, about 1967.

Actor Chief Dan George (center) during the filming of Spirit of the Wind, *a movie dramatization of Attla's early years.*

Bundled against the January cold, Attla competes in the annual Exxon Open in Anchorage in 1990.

Attla and his team compete in the Orville Lake Memorial championships in 1990.

Attla checks the condition of one of his huskies in the backyard of his North Pole, Alaska, home.

Chapter 17

Breeding Business

The dream team didn't last. Five dogs that had been part of the super team, including leaders Swift and Grover, died before the next Fur Rendezvous. Three of the dogs died in transit as they were being transferred out of Huslia. After being loaded into the airplane, freight was loaded onto their dog boxes and they suffocated. In another incident, George's kids were caring for his dogs, with Bobby Vent's help, when the two died mysteriously.

"They said they were fine in the morning, and in the evening they were dead," said Attla. No one ever figured out the cause of their deaths.

Dog mushing is a cyclical business. Some racing dogs have just one year of top-notch competition in them. They get hurt, fall ill, don't fit in with the mix of the rest of the team. Even when a team is raised and developed together, three years at the top is a long time. So a musher like Attla, who hoped to be a world championship contender year after year, was forced to constantly rebuild. It was an understood part of the sport, and it is not so different from other sports.

When Attla moved to North Pole, he changed more than location in his life. There was a time when Huslia was the dog capital of the world, but that time had passed. Now, the Fairbanks area was tops. Top mushers like Gareth Wright, Harvey Drake, Bill

Taylor, and Harold Greenway, the latter three all North American champions, were concentrated there.

"I had to rebuild again, but there were a lot of other mushers around, and dogs were cheap back then," said Attla.

He was able to buy six dogs from Gareth Wright for about nine hundred dollars. Today, of the sixty dogs Attla might have in his yard at a given time, only the bottom ten of those would go for as little as eight hundred dollars each. Clearly, the scope of the sport has also changed.

"A couple of years ago, I asked for twenty-five thousand dollars for one dog," said Attla. "I didn't get it." Lingo was perhaps the greatest dog Attla ever had. He asked for that much money, figuring that the man calling from Denmark would never pay the price. Lingo was long past his prime as a racing dog, but he had a reputation as an excellent stud dog.

"I told this guy, 'Yeah, every dog in my yard is for sale for a price,'" said Attla. "When I told him I wanted twenty-five thousand dollars, he said he'd call me back. I didn't think I'd hear from him again. He did call me back and said he couldn't afford it. But then he asked if I'd be interested in leasing Lingo for the winter. I leased him for five thousand dollars. I was pretty confident he wouldn't pay twenty-five thousand dollars to buy him."

Some years before that, when Lingo was still racing, a man from Switzerland visited Attla's fish camp on the Yukon River and said he wanted to buy the dog.

"We sat down and I said, 'Yeah, Lingo's for sale,'" said Attla. "I said that I needed a new boat and I'd take thirty-six thousand for Lingo. He didn't take Lingo."

Attla said the highest price he's ever heard paid for a leader is seven thousand dollars, and it was champion musher Charlie Champaine, not Attla, who made the sale. It was for a dog too old to run, too, he said.

The acquisition of six dogs for nine hundred dollars in 1972 was still a bargain. Although Wright had purchased the dogs from another musher and had a surplus, Attla was impressed with Wright's capabilities and thought he couldn't go wrong buying dogs from him.

"He was breeding these dogs he called Aurora huskies. I saw that the dogs he was breeding were faster than my own. They were faster going downhill and on level going, but mine maintained the same speed all the time. They would never give up, they wouldn't slow down on the uphills. I thought that they had a better work ethic, but I saw Gareth had some faster dogs."

Another time Attla spotted a dog he liked in Bill Taylor's team, but Taylor wanted three hundred dollars for the dog called Lonely, and Attla didn't want to pay it. By 1972, Wright had the dog and Attla got it from him. Lonely, a female, was bred to Scottie, one of Attla's old leaders, and two of the dogs that came out of that litter were among the best leaders Attla ever had. Freckles and Chris became stars.

It is always possible that a musher will breed one great dog by accident. There are always flukes of nature. But, for the most part, a musher won't get a litter of great pups by accident. It takes science and planning.

"You look for great bloodlines," said Attla, "and you also breed dogs by the way they think, by the way their minds work."

There are no guarantees, of course. A dog might still have a glaring weakness and not ever make it into the racing team. It might break down mentally; it might be a dog that gives up. Very few dogs, said Attla, are willing to run as hard as they can year after year. Their willingness to run often gives out before any physical problems arise, though like human racers, there's no planning for minor aches and pains. No musher can anticipate that one of his key dogs will harm itself by stumbling over a hole in the trail.

Every musher looks for different characteristics in dogs. After all, there is no one right way to win a championship.

Champion huskies must run fast—up to twenty miles per hour in races—and they must have the stamina to run that fast three days in a row. A George Attla dog wants to run, and will run even if it's not in the mood to run. It'll think it wants to run.

"Raising your own dogs," said Attla, "means raising dogs to fit your personality. All mushers want that, but different people have different personalities. My dogs wouldn't fit some people."

Always, of course, the musher is making judgments. Will this dog be good enough? If he thinks it is and he's wrong, he loses. If he thinks it isn't, and it really was, he often never finds out. This is art at least as much as science.

During the summer of 1991, Attla lent a dog to a young musher who took it from North Pole to his father's fish camp on the Yukon River. The dog had to travel by truck for more than a hundred miles, then by boat, then by land to get to the fish camp. It didn't like the journey.

"It turned out that it really didn't want to leave home," said Attla. "Some dogs get attached. I think it would kill them to be sold or given away to somebody. I've loaned dogs out that were too young. They get adjusted in time usually. The one on the Yukon will probably adjust. It's only two years old."

More than a decade had passed since Bobby Vent agreed that Attla was a real dog man. The times had changed, however, and being a real dog man meant, more than ever, breeding your own dogs. Dog suppliers were drying up all over the state; the snowmachine was now king. Building a team year by year now seemed impractical, and Attla recognized that he needed to build a kennel so that he would have a steady supply of reliable dogs he could count on season after season.

If a musher had dozens of dogs, though, he also had to feed dozens of dogs. And that cost money.

During the summer of 1973, Attla got lucky. A new bridge was going to be built on the Yukon River, and Attla seized the chance to put his piloting experience to work. He got a job guiding the boats up the river that were bringing in the construction materials, then he went to work on site as a supervisor. While he was out on the Yukon, he got a commercial fishing license and reaped a tremendous catch of salmon to feed his dogs.

For three years, he worked on the Yukon Bridge and fished, developing a market for the fish back in Fairbanks. Those summers, George worked two jobs simultaneously, and though that permitted him to boost his bank account when he was trying to buy dogs, it wore him out.

"I knew I was going to have to give something up," said Attla. "I kind of liked that paycheck coming in every weekend. You know how much money you're going to make. The fishing was completely different. You weren't too sure. By then I had a big walk-in freezer on the Yukon. I was storing fish in there during the week, and then I'd run it into town on the weekend. I was forever tired that summer."

Catching the fish saved Attla a fortune in food for the dogs, though, and he needed lots of food. "I was raising pups like mad," he said.

His dogs had forty pups that summer—quite a departure from the old days. The dogs really made the decision for him: if he quit fishing, how would he feed them? So he gave up his steady summer job to become a full-time fisherman.

"I had wanted to raise dogs for a long time, but I just couldn't do it," said Attla. "With that job on the Yukon Bridge, everything fell into place."

Not having to scrape around for dogs, Attla could always have enough good dogs to race a strong team in the Fur Rendezvous in February and come back with a strong team in the North American in March, too.

Mushers, like other athletes, are constantly learning how to improve. When Attla first competed in the Fur Rendezvous in 1958, sprint dogs were trained differently than they are now. Mushers believed in long-distance training. If the Rondy heats were twenty-five miles each, then they'd train their dogs with runs of thirty or forty miles. That produced dogs that were long on stamina but short on speed. It was nonspecific training. The dogs loped through the race, not extending themselves.

"They were paced down too much," said Attla. "They weren't real sprinters. They were fast dogs, but we didn't train them right according to today's methods."

Over time, it became apparent that it was trickier than it seemed to train the same dogs for both the Rondy and the North American. The Rondy was run into the woods, but the North American had more hills on the course, and wove around near the University of Alaska-Fairbanks campus. Although the Rondy had three heats of the same length, the North American had two twenty-mile heats followed by a longer, tougher segment of thirty miles.

"For the twenty-milers, you just go out and run them as hard as you can," said Attla. "The thirty-milers, you have to pace your dogs a little more. I think it helps them, actually, having those two twenty-milers. It slows them down so they can't go all out for the thirty-miler."

At first, the Rondy definitely meant more to Attla because the fans seemed more enthusiastic. In Anchorage, a dog team running through downtown was unique. At the North American in Fairbanks, the dogs were taken for granted because so many mushers lived in the area. Still, the North American became important to Attla over time.

When Attla developed the idea for his own kennel, he thought in terms of having enough good dogs available to carry him through both races, so that injuries wouldn't knock him out of contention.

Robert Attla believes his older brother owes his resourcefulness to growing up in the village and the difficulties he had to overcome in making a living for himself despite his leg. The same traits not only made George a champion racer, but also gave him the impetus to create his own dog yard, Robert thinks. "It was almost unbelievable that a person could make it with a kennel," said Robert. "It was almost unheard of. He turned the kennel into his livelihood. Everybody else's kennel was an expense."

When Attla won the Fur Rendezvous in 1958, Robert was proud, but he never thought it would become his brother's whole life.

"None of us realized what that was leading up to," he said. "A career? No. You know, the type of life we led in the village, to come back a cripple just about made him a misfit. The way we made our living back then, we'd spend all day snowshoeing. We were on our feet the whole time. But George had too much drive to sit around. His leg didn't seem to hold him down that much. He had the drive to make up for it, which I really thought was rare.

"Another person would sit back and live on welfare. He just wasn't that type. I was amazed he was able to make it into a year-round thing. Back then, there were really only two races a year, the Fur Rendezvous and the North American. What were you going to do with the dogs the rest of the year? But he did it. It has come a long way."

Making a kennel work twenty years ago was, as Robert Attla said, virtually unheard of. There were no smooth-running, well-known operations for Attla to pattern himself after. Just as he had to gain much of his knowledge about racing dogs from his own experiences, he had to learn as he went along, building his kennel.

Before, if Attla made an error in judgment about a dog, he could give it away to someone who wanted it as a pet, or he could sell it and try to buy another. Now, more than ever, he had to rely on his own expertise. Since he didn't have time to train all his dogs and then weed out the weakest, Attla was forced to make a call on each dog's capability at a younger age.

"The number-one way to know that you've got a good dog," said Attla, "is to watch the way they jump—the way their gaits are when they jump. I can't really tell until I get them in harness, so they have to be five or six months old. I get a clue then on whether they'll have the right gait for the team. That's important because you can't change the gait of a dog. What they start out with is their natural running style, and if they don't jump right that first time, they're never gonna jump right."

The Attla test involves putting the young dog in harness, climbing on the back of a sled and shouting, "Go!" How that dog responds at that moment is critical to his racing career. "If he jumps, and his back line is still smooth when he comes down, and there's no jerk in the tug line, just a smooth motion, then he has a smooth gait," said Attla. "You can't teach that. A dog either has it or he doesn't have it. You can tell instantly whether that dog is going to be good and fit into the kind of team you want."

All dogs are trainable, Attla thinks, but they may not be trainable for a championship team. After his first impression, Attla will try to trade the dog away. But if he sees what he likes in a dog, then the work begins. Winning, in dogs as well as in humans, is a state of mind, he believes. A dog with a smooth gait has physical potential. The next step is to determine if the dog has mental potential.

"Is his mind strong enough to be a champion? The young dog will force himself to run if he's tough," said Attla. "Those older dogs are going to run, and then the pup has to run with them. If his mind isn't strong enough, he's gonna think, 'Well, the hell with this, this is too tough,' and he's gonna start dragging. He'll throw himself on his back and start dragging and say, 'No, I'm not gonna do this. It's too hard.'"

That dog gets shipped out. But the pups that try to keep up with the older dogs are keepers.

"Even if they don't want to do it, even if they can't, they'll try," said Attla. "Those are the ones worth working with. Those are the ones with potential."

Chapter 18

Working Dogs

Spotty was the first important lead dog Janet Clarke bought in the mid-Eighties. It came from George Attla when it was seven years old. Clarke was looking to move up in class and break into open racing in the Fur Rendezvous, and she wanted a dog that would get her around the course. She had no illusions yet of challenging him for the title.

That winter, she was competing in a race at Montana Creek about a hundred miles from Anchorage. Attla was also in the race. Somehow, Spotty got loose from Clarke's team and romped along the trail. But instead of running off into the woods, the dog chased after Attla, caught him from behind, and pranced alongside as Attla crossed the finish line. "Just for old time's sake," laughed Clarke.

It was not one of Attla's better days, and afterward he joked, "I knew things were going bad when I was being caught by my own old leader."

Clarke, a schoolteacher from Eagle River, just outside downtown Anchorage, began mushing in the early Eighties. Like so many other mushers who gradually move up in class from the three-dog events to the open class, she was told George was the man to see when she wanted better dogs.

Buying Spotty, a dog she knew had run well for Attla, gave her the feeling that she was getting somewhere.

"It was a shot of confidence just to have a dog like that," said Clarke. "I would say that if you took a sampling of all of the mushers, there would be a general consensus; no one can get what George can get from a team. He just knows more about dogs than all of us who intellectualize about it."

In the winter of 1992, when Clarke had her breakthrough race, finishing third in the world championship, she was thinking of her team's ancestors. "For so many of us," she said, "when we look at the lineage of our dogs, when we look back and see the great ones, most of them came from George Attla."

Long before 1992, the Attla dog yard had developed into the General Motors assembly line of sprint dogs. From the glimmering of an idea that the kennel could supply him with new dogs year after year, the kennel had grown into such an impressive operation that it could supply any musher who needed dogs with replacements. Need a leader? Call George. Need a wheel dog? Call George. Need a team dog? Call George. Of course, you had to understand that George was keeping the best talent for himself.

When a musher bought a dog, he was not only buying the animal, he was buying its pedigree. And that also meant he was buying a dog raised by George Attla, trained by George Attla, or at the least, bred by George Attla. George Attla dogs became the brand name of the business.

Fifteen years after his first Rondy, Attla knew what he was looking for in a husky. Physically, a sprint dog should be only fifty pounds and, ideally, just under that, so they aren't dragging too much weight, but have the strength to run hard for three days. A forty-seven- or forty-eight-pound dog may be perfect.

Once Attla has decided a dog has the right stuff physically and mentally, he develops it carefully. Any dog younger than two years old is probably too young to race. There's too great a risk of injury.

"They're bound to pull a muscle," he said. "Even in two-year-olds, that happens. Once you get to a two-year-old, though, you pretty much should know if that dog is going to make it. Some of them still quit. They crack and think, 'I can't do this. I'm in way over my head.'" The musher must be a mind reader. It's an iffy proposition.

The perfect age for the whole team is three years old. By that age, the only thing being tested is its willingness to keep going. The training begins with short runs, and as the dogs age, their mileage goes up so that they are being challenged but not overburdened. By the time they are asked to run sixteen miles at a time—a common distance in races other than the big two—a dog is either going to run or not going to run.

The dogs that reach the point of running that far in ideal conditions, say twenty-degree temperatures, are then pushed to do more, to prove that they are not just acceptable running dogs, but championship dogs. Attla will take those dogs on the same sixteen-mile run when it's warm out, perhaps forty-five degrees.

"If you want to give a dog a test, run him sixteen miles when it's really hot," said Attla. "And you'll see right there if he can make it in the Rendezvous or not. A few three-year-olds, even, will say the heck with it. They'll show you signs that they don't feel like running hard. Any dog that shows you a sign like that, refusing to pull his weight, is showing you that he can't make it as a champion. He's showing you that somewhere along the line he's gonna quit.

"Very seldom is it a physical problem that weeds a dog out of my team. It's usually mental. If the thought enters his head even one time that it's too tough to run, somewhere along the line he's gonna say, 'To hell with you,' and I'll be out of luck."

Although there are some mushers who might believe George Attla can talk with his dogs, Attla is actually searching for signals.

"It's just little things that you look for," he said. "Some of them are so small. Like he might look off to the side. Or he might lean a little toward the other dogs in a position he's not supposed to be in."

Signs of weakness. There's no room for weakness in the Attla team, just as there was little tolerance of weakness back in the village when the winters were rugged and food had to be put on the table. By the time an Attla dog is ready for racing in the Fur Rendezvous, it will have covered three thousand miles, including approximately seven hundred in the season leading up to the race.

Summers are easy for the dogs. They truly have a dog's life—eating, lying around in the sun. It's vacation time. The hard work, peaking for the big races, begins about the third week in September, before the snow falls.

The first running experience for most Attla dogs is often on dirt trails, pulling four-wheeled recreational vehicles. After the laid-back summer, the first runs are only three miles. Trails lead right out Attla's backyard into the woods that connect into a main trail system running near the Alaska pipeline; its silvery metal gleams in the sunshine and weaves through open spaces and forests of birch and aspen.

The selection of the third week of September to start training did not come by happenstance. All steps in the development of the kennel and racing were by trial and error. At one time Attla started heavy mileage programs in November. It didn't work.

"They have to have miles on them to be in the best physical shape by a certain time," said Attla. "I want them to peak for the Rendezvous and North American. If you start in November, you pile the miles on and they may be in better physical shape, but they're mentally disturbed. They get to a stage where they don't want to train. They're burned out. If you do it for a longer period of time, adding miles, then they don't mind it."

Attla could control the training program, but one thing neither he nor any other musher can control is the natural evolution of great dogs. Just as environment, upbringing, training, coaching, and opportunity combine to create the most advantageous conditions for a human champion athlete to perform, dogs given the same conditions are expected to perform the same way. Yet in both instances, there is no accounting for intangibles. Will, desire, and heart are all characteristics of champions, but only the athlete knows how deep the supply runs.

"Sometimes a super litter of pups makes for great champions," said Attla. "You don't know when that litter is going to come along. Your next litter could be your great litter, but you don't know if that's gonna happen."

The move from three-mile runs to sixteen-mile runs is marked by intermediate steps. By the time the dogs are up to nine miles at a stretch, there is almost always snow on the ground in North Pole. That's mid-October, when in much of the rest of the United States the fall foliage is just beginning.

"When it gets a little colder and when the snow comes, they're just as happy as they can be. Their attitude really improves. It's interesting. Sled dogs, and dogs in general, are smarter than most people give them credit for. You hook them to a four-wheeler and you've really got control. You can stop them. Then you hook them to a sled when they're in good shape and you have a runaway.

"They're sliding along, and they know you don't have control of them. They take advantage of you. They hit a really rough area and they try to throw you off. No kidding. They'll run as fast as they can through the rough area and then look back to see if you're still there. So they know what's going on."

Over the years, Attla has observed an evolution in sprint mushing dogs that mirrors the evolution of the human culture they've been part of. The dogs he first raced in the villages and brought to big races in Anchorage and Fairbanks were dogs that never quit. Since then, he said, dogs have gotten softer because they're not used for work.

"The dogs I came out of the village with in 1972 were dogs who never thought, 'This is too tough,'" said Attla. "They worked traplines. They hauled firewood. They got that attitude from the people who were handling them. The people in the village, if they had to walk twenty hours on a pair of snowshoes, they didn't think, 'It's too far, I can't do it.' They just went ahead and did it.

"Now if you walk twenty miles on snowshoes, it's because you want to do it, but you don't have to. But why do it? It's too tough.

You don't want to do it. If you live in the city, why walk? Take the bus. The people who taught dogs then were tougher than they are today. The first dogs I had from the village, their leg would have to be broken before they'd ride in to the finish line in the basket, or they'd have to be really exhausted. If you crossed the finish line with a dog in the basket, he was passed out. He was sleeping. They would give you full, honest effort. They wouldn't quit on the job."

Dogs that have grown up in the city with a comparatively pampered lifestyle may be better pure athletes who can run faster, but they aren't as tough as their predecessors, said Attla. And he wonders if he's as tough as he used to be, too, since he grew accustomed to city ways, watching television and driving a truck into town.

"You take today's dogs," said Attla, "and if you are a spectator at a race, almost all the teams come in with dogs in the basket of the sled. They're sitting up and looking at the scenery. They're not exhausted. They quit before that. The musher and the dog are the same. It's what you passed down to your dogs. I have gotten a little softer and I'm not as demanding as I used to be, I guess. It's today's people."

When George Attla wants a cup of coffee today, he walks across his kitchen to the pot on the stove and pours one. The refrigerator hums in the background. His daughter watches television nearby. The washing machine shakes in the other room. His entire way of life has changed from the days in Huslia—except for the dogs.

"Life is easier, for both humans and dogs," said Attla.

One thing that was never easy, though, as Attla built his kennel and his team, was winning world championships.

The first Rendezvous after Attla moved to North Pole was the 1973 race. That was won by Carl Huntington, Sidney's son, who twenty years later is still the only musher to have won both the world championship of sprint dog mushing and the Iditarod Trail Dog Race. Gareth Wright finished second, Roland Lombard third, and Attla fourth. Attla was eleven minutes behind Huntington.

One by-product of Attla's kennel expansion was the shrewd

strategy of buying up village dogs as they were abandoned. Huntington relied on the use of some leased village dogs to fill out his team, much as Attla had done in the past. Jim Welch thinks Attla's purchasing plan was at least partially focused on keeping top dogs away from Huntington.

"Carl had a core of dogs himself and leased others," said Welch. "George bought up a lot of dogs that Carl had leased and sold them places where Carl couldn't get at them. George has known for a long time that the competition is not just on the race track."

A year later, the Sixties were revisited in the Seventies. Doc Lombard, still adding trophies to the mantel, bested Attla by forty-three seconds. The two men were almost ten minutes ahead of third place.

So even with the move to North Pole, Attla wasn't closing the gap, he was still falling further behind Lombard. At the end of the 1974 sprint mushing campaign, Roland Lombard owned eight world championships, and George Attla owned four.

No one would have guessed that Lombard had won his final title and Attla, then forty years old, would still be a force in the sport two decades later.

Chapter 19

Iditarod!

People said they were crazy. People said it couldn't be done. Mush from Anchorage to Nome? Mush across Alaska?

In the winter of 1973, amid great expectation and equal skepticism, the Iditarod was born. The longest dog race of all time, to be run in probably the harshest conditions. This was an expedition with a clock on it and with a fifty-thousand-dollar payoff at the end.

The moment George Attla heard about the Iditarod, he planned to race. He figured he had the best dogs in the world, so if any dogs could make it over eleven hundred miles of tough terrain, his could.

Attla had sprint dogs, but twenty years ago no one had long-distance racing dogs, because there weren't any long-distance races. Obviously, sprint dogs couldn't keep up their race pace for more than a thousand miles. Stamina would be needed.

Joe Redington of Knik was the inventor of the race that has since become the most popular and closely followed mushing event in the world. He started it to revive Alaska's interest in dogs. As Redington traveled around the state, he was saddened to see communities forsaking their traditional use of dogs for snowmachines. He hoped that a race that captured the imagination of the public would create more mushers and focus more attention on Alaska's heritage. He succeeded beyond his wildest dreams. Joe Redington never thought the Iditarod would be televised on national networks, that's for sure.

The historical peg for the race was the diphtheria serum run of 1925, when courageous mushers battled frigid conditions to bring medicine to Nome. The route itself was an old mail trail that cut through villages, old mining camps, and the ghost town of Iditarod. Originally, Redington wanted the race to go from Anchorage to Iditarod, about five hundred miles, but when he was told no one would care because no one had heard of Iditarod, he said, "Hell, let's go to Nome then. Everyone's heard of Nome."

Indeed, everyone had heard of Nome, a gold rush town that at the turn of the century had attracted such characters and entrepreneurs as Marshal Wyatt Earp and legendary boxing promoter Tex Rickard, the man who built Madison Square Garden. Yes, the nation remembered Nome.

The dogs that were racing in 1973 were all sprint dogs, but Redington had a simple answer for anyone who doubted that dogs could run so far. Thinking of the way the mail was delivered in years past, he said, "They've done it before, so why can't they do it again?"

Attla wanted to be part of the Iditarod. The prize money was nice—twelve thousand dollars—but the adventurous aspect of the Iditarod appealed most to him. For that matter, even if Redington was promising big money, most of the mushers who set out from downtown Anchorage weren't convinced the money would be there at the end. No, the initial Iditarod spirit was the chance to be part of something that was new, not to make a profit.

"We didn't know if we'd get there," said Attla. "I had my own doubts. There was an old guy named Chief Henry. One of my brothers went to talk to him, and he said it couldn't be done. There were some older people around who didn't think you could make a thousand miles. I was looking for the experience, the country you were going to see, and I actually thought I could win the race. I had the confidence."

There were some familiar names in the first Iditarod besides Attla. Bobby Vent, then in his late sixties, entered. So did Herbie Nayokpuk, the "Shishmaref Cannonball," and Dick Mackey. Most of the thirty-four starters were mushers who'd made names for themselves in big sprint races or in village races.

Mackey, who helped Redington organize the race and eventually finished seventh, said there was a special feeling surrounding the first Iditarod. There was excitement but also uncertainty as mushers lined up to attempt to do something never tried before. "You will never be able to duplicate the feeling of the first one," said Mackey. "Wives and sweethearts were down at the starting line in tears because here we were going off into the wilds, never to be seen again."

Not quite. In fact, the mushers were seen and heard from often because the race captured the attention of the state immediately. Fans followed reports from the trail with an astonishing level of eagerness. Attla thinks much of their interest centered on the question of whether it could even be done. People—even veteran mushers—put themselves in the position of the racers and shook their heads. They couldn't imagine mushing such a distance. If there was a problem raising prize money, there definitely was no problem raising interest. People loved the historical link and the challenge of the elements.

There was a thousand-dollar prize for the first musher to cover the sixty miles from Anchorage to Knik, and Attla, who took the early lead, was going after it. He was surprised when Isaac Okleasik of Teller, who ultimately finished in sixth place, passed him two miles outside Knik.

"That doggone Isaac caught me up there," said Attla. "I said, 'Holy cow, there goes a thousand dollars.' He just shot away. So there went a thousand bucks, and then I thought that was probably the only money we were going to make."

There is now two decades' worth of long-distance mushing experience and lore for a beginner to draw upon if he chooses to enter the Iditarod. But in 1973, the mushers were doing everything for the first time.

These mushers were driving dogs that had been trained for sprints or for work around the cabin. They had heavy freight sleds—the kind gold-rush claimants used to carry their goods into the country—not the streamlined, lightweight sprint mushing sleds commonly employed. After all, the mushers were heading off into the teeth of an Alaskan winter and there was no telling what they might need for survival.

There was a lot of confusion about feeding. What was the best kind of food? No one really knew. How many calories did the dogs burn up in a day? Now it's estimated that an Iditarod dog burns seven thousand or more calories a day while racing. Back then, no one had a clue.

At one time, it had been common to feed sprint dogs rice, fish, and moose meat, a little of everything. There had been a move toward emphasizing more commercial dog food, though, and the stuff then in use for short races didn't do the job on the trail in the Iditarod. The harder the dogs worked, the more they blew through the food. Some of the teams weakened, and twelve of the mushers dropped out.

"My dogs were starving," said Attla. "I was giving them good food, but they were starving. They were using up so many calories."

The day after Okleasik took the Knik prize, Attla passed him back and retook the lead. That night, when he made camp, Vent joined him, but Dick Wilmarth passed them all before dawn.

In 1992, Martin Buser of Big Lake broke the eleven-day barrier in the Iditarod, winning the twentieth-anniversary race in ten days, nineteen hours, seventeen minutes. The first racers weren't nearly so quick. The first few Iditarods have been described by mushers and other observers as long camping trips.

"We traveled only in the daytime," said Attla. "I got up at two o'clock in the morning to get ready. I wanted to make camp for the day before dark so that I could gather wood and build a fire."

These days it's rare for mushers to sleep more than a few hours at a time the entire race, except for their mandatory twenty-four-hour and six-hour layovers. During the first Iditarod, mushers traveled together and made camp together, and it was more of a social race.

For a while, though, Attla kept opening distance between his team and the others. By McGrath, a checkpoint roughly four hundred miles into the race, he had a twenty-four-hour lead. However, he also had a weary dog team. A friend of his, Nick Miller, was there when he pulled in, and when Attla complained that he couldn't figure out the right way to feed his dogs, Miller said, "Hey, how long do you think you'd last on a box of cornflakes?" Attla resolved to add more substantial food to the diet.

Attla recognized that his dogs also needed a long rest, so he bedded down in McGrath until Wilmarth, Vent, and Dan Seavey caught up. When they were ready to go, he joined them. Army personnel rode snowmachines to clear the trail, but not even dedicated sweeping can keep a path open in Alaska when the wind starts howling and the snow starts blowing. The Iditarod had its first major storm. First of many. Since then, vicious storms have become part of the folklore of the race, playing a part in the outcome more than once.

Checkpoints were spaced much farther apart in the first Iditarod than they are now, one reason sleds were heavier to pull. They had to carry more supplies. On the third day out of McGrath, headed for Ruby two hundred-fifty miles away, the mushers got lost—a dangerous situation if only because they were also running out of dog food. At one point, said Attla, the mushers spied moose tracks and considered leaving the trail to shoot and eat it.

This demanding stretch killed Attla's chances of winning the race. He limped into Ruby with hungry, tired, and ailing dogs. One dog died there, and he dropped several others. By Galena, another fifty miles farther on, pneumonia was sapping the energy of his remaining dogs.

"I knew I couldn't go on," said Attla. "They were so run down, I didn't think they had the strength to fight the cold. I brought them inside a friend's house, fed them every six hours, and got hold of some penicillin from a health aide."

The great adventure of the Iditarod didn't seem like fun at this point. "I was losing interest," said Attla. "I enjoyed the camping out, though. I was young enough that the cold didn't bother me that much. And it was fun coming into the villages with a dog team. It was almost like turning back the clock."

Attla was down to six dogs after starting the race with fourteen. But with rest and care, the remaining dogs perked up, and after two days, he resumed racing.

Wilmarth, Vent, and Seavey, the eventual one-two-three finishers, were far ahead by then. Three others were a day ahead, and five more teams were pulling into Galena when he left.

The six rejuvenated dogs just blasted along, picking off teams one by one. They behaved as if they were at the start of a race rather than seven hundred miles into one. Attla covered the ninety miles between Kaltag and Unalakleet without a long break.

"That's the longest run I've ever made in my life," he said. "Those six dogs were in terrific shape. Especially one dog, a dog called James. He was barking and happy; he wasn't even tired after ninety miles. He was not the fastest, but he was a really tough animal. He must have been a dumb one, too, because he didn't know how hard it was to do what he'd done."

Attla placed fourth in the first Iditarod, crossing the finish line on Front Street in Nome twenty-one days, eight hours, and forty-seven minutes after leaving Anchorage. Attla won four thousand dollars. Wilmarth won in twenty days, forty-nine minutes. The final musher, John Schultz, didn't arrive in Nome until more than thirty-two days after the race had begun. In comparison with the times recorded today, it *was* a camping trip. But there was tremendous satisfaction in finishing. This was one case where the journey itself was meaningful.

"To be part of it was.., hell's bells," said Mackey. "I'd rather have done that than been President of the United States."

When the race was over, Redington, who had mortgaged his house to help raise the prize money, addressed the mushers and asked them if they wanted to have another one. They cheered wildly, and so he pledged to put on a bigger and better Iditarod the next year. Over time, the Iditarod has eclipsed the Fur Rendezvous and North American in the public eye. It has indeed become bigger and better every year.

"I never thought it would go on again," said Attla. "But it sure caught on. It turned into a big event all right. I was happy about completing the race. It didn't look so good there for a while in the middle. It didn't look as if the dogs could make it. They looked terrible. I'd never seen dogs in that condition."

Attla was glad he did the Iditarod, was pleased to finish it, but not satisfied—he didn't win. Any race Attla entered he expected to win.

Once, at the starting line of the North American, Jim Welch witnessed a scene that stuck in his mind and gave him insight into just how intensely George Attla burns to win. This was in the Seventies, during the period when Carl Huntington's dogs seemed to be the best. George's brother Robert surveyed the competition with him. Welch heard Robert tell George, "You're racing for second." "Something clicked inside him." said Welch. "You could see it in his eyes. They grew more intense. He doesn't race for second."

Proud to be part of the first Iditarod, Attla couldn't shake the nagging feeling that he could have won. So he entered the Iditarod again in 1974.

The weather in the second Iditarod, won by Carl Huntington, was far more brutal than the year before. In places, the racers faced a windchill factor of a hundred below zero. Attla dropped out of the race in Galena while traveling with the lead pack.

"My dogs had frozen their feet," he said. "Some of them were frozen all the way up to their shoulders. Those dogs were still willing to go, but I couldn't stand the idea of the punishment I'd be giving them. To go on you have to be able to see your dogs run and watch them put their feet down and leave blood behind. You've got to be able to live with that kind of stuff."

So Attla's second Iditarod ended in disappointment, and he never entered the race again. "I never enjoyed doing the Iditarod that much," said Attla. "The idea of staying up for say, fifty hours, and getting tired to the point where you're imagining things, to me that's not fun. You're only going to live once. If it's not enjoyable, then don't do it."

Sprint mushing was still George's sport; winning the Iditarod was not his primary goal. No, Attla's main goal was still to win more Fur Rendezvous world championships than Doc Lombard.

Chapter 20

Resilience

The light was a sharp, piercing knife. Even the tiniest ray of light pricked his eyes with a stunning violence. No light. No light. No light. For two weeks, George Attla sat in the dark of his trapping cabin, eyes closed to the outside world. He was snow-blind.

One day in the late Fifties, George, his brother Steven, Georgie Yatlin, and Tony Sam were out trapping. They stayed out for twelve hours on a brilliantly sunny day in March in search of beaver. The powerful sunlight reflected off the whiteness of the snow, and by that evening, Attla could see nothing at all.

The next morning, he couldn't even step outdoors. Any glint of sun shot sparks of pain through his eyes. Attla was a prisoner in the cabin. Two weeks should have been long enough to recuperate, but a strange growth appeared on Attla's right eye. Tony Sam took a piece of thin, delicate cigarette paper and scraped off the growth.

Attla thought he was going to be all right. A man with only one good leg could sure use two good eyes. But his right eye never healed properly, and as time passed, his vision blurred. He ignored it. George got headaches. He ignored them. Finally, after years of aggravation and deterioration, he went to the doctor.

The diagnosis was glaucoma, a disease that creates internal pressure on the eyeball. Left untreated, it results in a hardening of the eyeball, erosion of sight, and eventually, blindness.

Attla never missed a racing season, but in the off-seasons of the late Sixties he had two operations. Both of the medical procedures necessitated taking long journeys. The doctors told him he had waited too long to have his problem checked out. The operations failed, and by the early Seventies, Attla was blind in one eye.

"I knew I had a problem," said Attla. "I just never took the time to do anything about it. Living so far from doctors, it was always a big trip. I don't know what I was thinking. I think a lot of men have that problem, that they're too macho. We don't check things out before it's too late. It was already too late for me."

The experience with his eye was not the only health problem Attla faced. Over a period of about eight years, between 1968 and 1976, Attla had to wonder exactly why his body was falling apart, behaving like an old car with a long-expired warranty.

During the summer of 1968, George developed a bleeding ulcer. He started hemorrhaging while he was working as a riverboat pilot, and he had to be carried off the boat. It was the final week of the season, nearing the time for the startup of training, when Attla underwent surgery. Part of his stomach was cut away, and he still sports a distinctive slash on his belly. He was slow to recover, and his rest interfered with his training regimen. "My stomach was still tender," he said. "I couldn't stand on the back of the sled. I could hardly train at all."

In early 1974, Attla had a gall bladder operation. He was in so much pain during the Fur Rendezvous and North American, he let his dogs do all the work.

That would seem to be enough intestinal disorders for anyone. But in 1976, about three weeks before the Fur Rendezvous, Attla's appendix burst, and he needed emergency surgery. Attla has a fuzzy memory of passing out during a training run near his North Pole home and waking up in the hospital when the operation was all over.

Talk about a training disruption. That kind of illness can be life-threatening. Attla thought of it merely as race-threatening.

"All the other mushers were out training," he said. "I didn't think 1 was going to be able to race the Rendezvous. I figured the problem wasn't going to go away by the time the race started. But I didn't lay around that long. I was in really good shape before I got sick. The only thing I was afraid of, going into the race, was that the sled would flip over and I wouldn't be able to hang on. I couldn't stretch my arms out."

If the sled tipped over, Attla wouldn't be able to control it. He would risk being dragged by his arms across the rough ground, causing excruciating pain. Attla was willing to take that gamble.

Attla let his oldest son, Gary, who was then in high school, race the dog team in the Exxon Open in Anchorage, the biggest world championship prelim. He won the race. That showed Attla his dogs were winners, anyway. Then dad took over for the big race.

"I just had such fantastic dogs that I won the Rendezvous," said Attla. "I didn't do anything physically. I don't think I pushed at all. I just kind of rode it out. My team was such a superior dog team."

In the middle of this series of physical calamities, Attla married for the second time. He met Karen when she was a spectator at a race. He talked her into becoming a volunteer handler, then later his wife. They had one child together, then divorced in 1982.

Except for this newfound love, Attla had to wonder if he was jinxed any time he walked away from a racecourse.

Terrible things may have been happening to Attla's body, but he was making great things happen on dog tracks all over the state. This was his payoff for his good judgment buying, training, and raising dogs.

The living room of Attla's North Pole home features rows of gleaming trophies. So does the hallway. And a nearby trailer is overflowing with others. A visit to Attla's homestead is akin to visiting the sprint mushing hall of fame. History is on display in every room.

The mementos themselves are souvenirs for Attla. They remind him of where he's been and where he hopes to go again. Just a glance at a trophy with its engraved date brings the memory of the race and of that particular dog team alive for him once more. Attla rarely differentiates between his world championships, but the 1975 team has a special place in his heart. "That," he said, "was a great litter of pups."

Freckles, a leader, was a dog with a lot of heart, according to Attla, and that is the highest compliment he can pay a dog. Freckles was a light red dog with blue eyes and a fiery spirit.

As the years have passed and Attla has grown older, one of the most consistent observations made about him is that he seems never to physically age. Except for the salt in his thick hair and in the mustache and tiny goatee he has grown over the years, Attla looks almost identical to the young man who first came out of the village.

Gareth Wright has joked more than once of Attla's longevity: "He even looks the same."

"Exactly," said Janet Clarke. "He seems to project a younger image. Everyone else is aging and he just seems to sit still."

Few realize just how remarkable that is, given all the traumas that Attla's wiry body has suffered over the years. All of those woes would likely have driven a lesser man into retirement, but Attla endured. He played the hand he was dealt each time. If he felt cheated, he never said so.

"You know, losing an eye and stuff, it's never bothered me," he said. "I've never thought of it as a handicap. Just like my leg. I never considered that a handicap. Yes, I've lost a race by less than ten seconds, but I've never thought I've lost because I'm crippled and couldn't run as fast by the sled. I couldn't run as fast, but that's not why I lost."

Tuberculosis, glaucoma, major operations. Attla has shrugged them all off. Incredibly, the most painful injury he ever had, the most annoying, depressing injury of all, and the one that most interfered with his efforts in the Fur Rendezvous, was, of all things, a finger injury. He tore off the top part of his right pinky.

Attla was training on the trails near home during the winter of 1984 and was attempting to invent a new sled brake. The contraption had a pair of hinges, and if the dogs ran the wrong way on a trail, Attla reached down, grabbed the brake, and jerked it back— only he caught his finger between the hinges and nearly chopped off the top third of it.

Strangely, the finger didn't bleed at all, but Attla rushed home and tied up the dogs. Inside the house, he gently removed his glove and saw his finger barely hanging by sinew. He drove to a clinic, and the doctor sewed the finger back on. It was hoped the reconstructive surgery would take and the nerves would regenerate. Attla, by now having learned some lessons about the advisability of medical visits, had his finger checked regularly.

A cold snap battered North Pole, so Attla loaded his dogs up in the truck and drove to Knik, about sixty miles north of Anchorage, for his final Rondy training. While in Knik, he followed instructions and had his finger checked every other day. The pain in the finger was intense. Instead of healing, it was hurting more and more.

The doctors kept telling Attla it was okay, the finger was improving. But it wasn't. He was sure it was infected. The doctors changed the bandages but detected no serious problem. There were some rough callouses that built up over time from holding sled handlebars, and somehow that area did get infected.

"It got so doggone badly infected that I could smell that finger," said Attla.

Attla was suspicious of being taken for a ride by doctors who didn't seem to be helping him. Every visit cost him fitly dollars, and he was feeling worse all the time. He was staying at Bill Sturdevant's house, and at night he talked more about the pain the finger was causing him than the upcoming race.

"I told him, 'Hey, I think my finger's badly infected. It's messing up my whole system.' I took the bandage off and started feeling around, and sure enough the finger seemed dead. Mentally, that really bothered me that my finger was dead."

Attla called the doctor at the clinic and told him he wanted the finger cut off. He went to the hospital in nearby Palmer for what Attla figured was going to be a ten-minute procedure. He was told to get in his pajamas, get in bed, and get ready for some tests.

"I said, 'Hey, wait a minute,'" said Attla. "'All I want you to do is to take this finger off. It's already dead, you know. All you've got to do is pull it off' and throw it away and send me on my way.'" Then they told him the operation would cost him a thousand dollars.

"I said, 'No way. I could buy a dog for that,'" he said.

So Attla put his clothes back on, got in the car, and went to the Alaska Native Medical Center in Anchorage. Doctors there cut off the top third of the finger in the emergency room.

"That's all there was to it," he said.

Only that wasn't all there was to it. The infection didn't disappear with the finger. The infection had already spread throughout his body. Two days before the Fur Rendezvous, Attla had to be admitted to the hospital and was put on intravenous feeding tubes.

After a day of treatment, he checked out, quietly went back to Knik, and made his final preparations for the race.

"I didn't tell anyone what was going on," he said.

On the morning of the first day of the race, February 10, Attla made a secret stop at the hospital. Over the years, there has been more and more negative publicity about athletes who abuse drugs, and although a comparatively benign painkiller seems minor compared with the cocaine addiction stories that emanate from professional sports leagues, Attla was skittish lest anyone discover what he was up to. He took a shot of Novocaine to deaden the feeling in his hand before the race began and, for the remaining two days of the race, repeated the procedure.

Weakened by the shock of the surgery, the infection, and the illness, and disturbed by the entire episode, Attla had the worst Fur Rondy of his career. The first day he was in the thick of the pack in fifth place, but each subsequent day he slowed more and more.

"I couldn't do hardly anything with that hand," said Attla. "I didn't have the full strength. It was hard to hold on to the sled."

He ended up in thirteenth place, more than twenty-seven minutes behind winner Charlie Champaine.

"Losing the finger, and it wasn't even the whole finger, bothered me more than anything that's ever happened to me," said Attla. "I think it was like a piece of me dying. It could be it bothered me more than all those other things because I did it to myself. With my invention. That was the end of my big invention."

Another musher would have taken a year off from the race, would have skipped it and chalked it up to the reality of the moment. But Attla figured if he could walk, he could race. Whatever the circumstances of the time, when the Rondy came, Attla coped. His resilience is renowned. Many of the other mushers understand and know of the physical problems he's had, but they know that when Attla stands on his sled runners to race, he's a potential winner.

"You've got to be a man to beat George Attla," said long-time friend Marvin Kokrine, also of North Pole. "It ain't an easy thing to do to beat any kind of champion. He never cries about his problems. He's always trying. He doesn't bellyache about it. He finds a way to overcome what has to be overcome."

Time and again, that's exactly what Attla did through the late Sixties and the Seventies. If something could be fixed, he fixed it. If it couldn't be fixed, he adjusted. As long as he could put his body onto the sled, he would race. Winning wasn't guaranteed, but if he was in the race, he might make it happen.

"George has had his share of valleys, and each time he's bounced back," said Jim Welch. "He's come back time and time again. It's easy to give up. Dog mushing is full of excuses when you don't win. He's always been able to come back, no matter what's happened."

Wright wonders whether it hasn't been easier for Attla to continue than to quit mushing. Thinking back to how Attla made his place in the sport after overcoming the impediment of making a living with his fused kneecap in the village, he can understand why Attla would repeatedly fight back against any other obstacles that would prevent him from racing.

"He was looking for a niche in life," said Wright. "And then he figured, 'This is where I can excel with my handicap.' If it is one. That's his whole life. Even today he can't live without mushing."

It was not enough that young Attla had to find a way to make do with a stiff leg. Middle-aged Attla had to overcome blindness in one eye. Retire? Certainly not. Adapt? Yes.

"I just had to adjust to being able to see out of only one eye. It never was that important on the trail," said Attla. "When you're working with somebody, you have to remember you're blind on that side, because you might hit somebody with a club or something. When I'm hunting, I used to shoot right-handed and now I shoot left-handed. It hasn't limited me. I don't let it. I just adjusted. I've never had any problems. I can still see all I want to see."

Where George Attla came from, you didn't complain when things went wrong. You had to deal with them. You worked to make them better. This is a man whose father was running a dog team on a trapline and cutting his own firewood in the forest as a blind senior citizen. As long as Attla could see out of one eye, he could race.

When young Attla first attended the new village school in Huslia, there was a teacher who had only one arm. That didn't stop him from participating in rough play with the boys. Attla frequently wrestled with him, and he discovered that the man had just as much strength in his one arm as most men had in two. Attla was fascinated that this could be so, and it was a lesson he never forgot: strength came as much from the man's mind as from his body. It's apparent Attla has never forgotten that.

"George Attla always has a winning attitude. He'll never lose that," said his friend Rudy Demoski of Fairbanks, who has raced in the Iditarod several times and frequently worked as a handler for Attla in the Rondy. During his last years of Rondy racing, when Demoski lived in nearby Wasilla, Attla parked his dogs at Demoski's house between Anchorage heats.

For years, Demoski worshipped Attla from a distance as a hero for his achievements, and as a good role model for Natives. And when he got to know him, he felt the same way.

"I'd have to admit, he's still my hero," said Demoski. "I still call him my hero."

When he teasingly calls the racer hero to his face, though, Attla tells him, "Shut up."

Chapter 21

Leaders

Susan Butcher, the four-time winner of the Iditarod Trail Sled Dog Race, likes to tell a story about her first great leader, Tekla.

One day, she was mushing along the trail and reached an ice-covered river. The dog stopped. She urged him on. He started running again, but stopped again, clearly wanting her to take another trail. Every time she cajoled him, he'd run for a few yards, then veer the other way. She couldn't figure out what the problem was.

Butcher finally thought, "OK, we'll do it your way." Moments later, the ice collapsed with no weight on it at all. There were no visible signs that anything would have gone wrong. Tekla just sensed it. If the team had advanced, it would have fallen into frigid waters. Tekla probably saved Butcher's life.

Now that's leadership.

Stories of great, smart lead dogs in the wild are legion. But great leaders are just as important to a sprint dog team, even if they are running on groomed trails and don't often make life-and-death choices. They communicate with the musher. They anticipate what the musher wants and make it happen. The lead dogs carry out orders. It doesn't matter how much a dog musher knows. It doesn't matter how wise he is, or how tough he is. He can't get anywhere without good leaders.

One of the greatest of Attla's leaders was Freckles, the main dog in his championship teams of the mid-Seventies. Freckles was tougher than tree bark. This dog had heart, spirit, smarts, and a will to win. Freckles wanted to run so badly, she didn't know when to quit.

On the final day of the 1976 North American—the thirty-mile day—Attla had a large lead. An uneven trail had been plowed on the course instead of the usually smooth path. A tractor had done the plowing, and in one spot the blade was lifted, leaving a bumpy section. Freckles, the lead dog, stepped onto the bump and collapsed screaming.

Attla halted his sled, ran to the front of the team, and watched Freckles writhe in pain. At the time he couldn't figure out what had happened, and he wasn't sure what was wrong with the dog. There was no apparent injury, though there was clearly something terribly wrong. He unhooked Freckles, gathered her in his arms, put her into the sled basket, and resumed the race. Only Freckles wouldn't stay put. Being out of the race hurt her more than the mysterious injury. She barked in a frenzy and started gnawing on Attla.

"I said, 'Holy cow, I'm not going to fight you for thirty miles,'" said Attla.

So he put Freckles back in the team. Freckles had trouble running smoothly at first, but the longer the race went, the better she got. By the end of the heat, Freckles was the best dog in Attla's team. He thought she was cured of whatever had sidelined her.

But after the race, when Attla took the dog out of harness and lifted her up to her dog box in his truck, he saw that both of her front paws were swollen as big as balloons. It turned out Freckles had broken a bone in each front paw. She was essentially running on two broken hands.

"She finished the whole race," said Attla. "That's a tough dog. She had a good mind. I had a lot of admiration for her. But she was never able to run again. Both of her paws mended, and it wasn't as though she couldn't do it, but I think she lost trust in me. When a dog is totally trained, it is totally depending on you to take care of it. And if you don't, and you hurt one like that, and you work it, they lose trust in you. They never perform again because they've lost the faith you've built into them."

Once healed, Freckles ran with the other dogs, but she never regained her edge. She was never willing to stretch, to put herself on the line again. The memory of the pain was apparently too fresh.

Dogs like Freckles come along only once every several years, for some mushers perhaps once in a lifetime. And though a musher may be able to borrow, lease, or buy dogs from friends to build a quality team, most of the time the very best leaders are homegrown. And most of the time, too, it's the job of the musher to develop what's already there. Being a leader among dogs is just like being a leader among men: to a major extent it's a God-given gift.

"The good leaders, the unusual ones, are born lead dogs," said Attla. "They have the personality for it, the desire to please you. They have it or they don't. It's something that you don't put there. It's a matter of being the boss and having a good attitude doing it."

The first inkling that a husky could become a leader comes at about six months of age, when the dog is first run in harness. Sometimes a dog will be special in lead right from the start.

"Say you picked out six dogs from a litter of ten that might look like they're going to make it as racers," said Attla. "Then you start trying different ones in the lead, and once in a while, you'll hit this star. God, that's a leader. He was born that way. You didn't make that dog."

A dog with star quality wants to be in the front of the team. He's not shy. He likes being in the lead, taking the turns on the trail, choosing the right direction. He responds to the musher's commands, and he does it happily. It's a great day when a musher recognizes a leader with innate skills.

"I say, 'Wow, I've got it,'" said Attla. "I've got my star for that year. And then I baby that dog a little bit. I don't put it under a lot of pressure. But they don't always turn out, either. Some of them have the right attitude, but they don't have the speed. They have physical limits."

Some dogs are such natural leaders that they can run in no other spot in the team. If they aren't terrifically fast, they don't make the team, but sometimes their brains make up for the lack of pure speed.

"The biggest thing when I'm training a dog is that I'm training it to win races, not just to get in shape," said Attla. "I have a purpose. What I do is try to get an animal totally depending on me to make all the decisions. Whatever has to be done, I make the decisions, so they have all their confidence in me. I get them leaning on me. I raise them that way."

Over the months leading up to the race, George regulates the training. He knows how much energy is available. Although a leader must be smart, a sprint mushing leader will never be called upon to make as many decisions as a long distance husky traveling in open country.

"A long distance animal has to go at its own pace," said Attla. "He has to be relaxed about what he's doing. The sprint dog has no relaxing point. He's always got to be tuned in to whatever I'm telling him to do, to whatever decisions I make on how to burn his fuel. A long distance dog will be the real leader of the team. He'll pick the trail, find the right direction."

The perfect combination of brains and speed is extraordinarily rare. In his first thirty-five years of sprint mushing, Attla believes he had barely a half-dozen truly great leaders and perhaps fourteen dogs in all that he would consider unusually good. Out of how many? That's a number that can't be counted. Hundreds. Thousands.

Of all the dogs that came and went in Attla's team and dog yard, so very few had the magical gifts needed to lead a world championship team. Nellie, whom Attla sold to Doc Lombard, was his first great dog, Attla thinks. Scottie was next in the late Sixties. Trot and Freckles, the dual leaders who made his teams in the mid-Seventies unbeatable, are highly rated in Attla's personal hall of fame. Having two at the same time was all Attla needed to put distance between himself and the other mushers. "They were really a great pair of leaders," said Attla.

Grover and Swift were two dogs that hinted at greatness, but they died in the early Seventies before reaching their full potential.

After Freckles and Trot, Keys was Attla's next great dog. "He was a super athlete," said Attla, "but not a great leader. You never knew where you were going when he was in lead, but he had so much talent. He would win races for me. He won quite a few races for me in the late Seventies."

Keys, like Freckles, had a red coat, but he was much larger. Though he had great talent, he couldn't always be relied on to stay with the program. "He had a mind of his own," said Attla. "He was not really what you'd call a super lead dog when it came to minding the musher. But even when he got me off the trail, he was still able to win the race." Keys was on the winning teams of 1979 and 1981.

Eventually, Attla sold the dog to another musher. Mushing attracts dog lovers, but mushers soon learn that the sport is a business as well as an enthusiasm, and to stay in the business they love, they have to be practical. Just as there wasn't much room in the village for dogs that didn't work, there's little chance in the dog yard for a dog that doesn't run.

Nevertheless, over the long course of George Attla's career, he has allowed ten retired dogs the luxury of staying on in his dog yard. Freckles, once she suffered her injury, had that privilege. So did Chris, another of Attla's famous leaders. Trot would have been offered the opportunity, but Attla allowed friends in Eagle River to take him in as a pet.

"Keeping dogs that don't race is a continuing expense," said Attla. "You can't have too many around at the same time. Retirement is pretty rare, only for pretty special dogs."

The best of the best, though, may have been a dog that didn't win as many races for Attla as his other top leaders, but one that gave an honest day's work and won races with inferior teams.

There is only one dog who has his portrait hanging on the wall in Attla's house, and that's Lingo. One of Attla's friends painted the picture of the dog for which Attla had once asked twenty-five thousand dollars.

Lingo led a team that won one world championship and one North American in the early Eighties, but he shouldered the weight of the whole team. With a veteran musher calling upon all his wiles, and a super leader that could lift a team beyond its apparent capabilities, Attla and Lingo made quite a pair.

"Of all the dogs I've had, Lingo is the dog that's done the most, not winning, but performing, and being able to produce good dogs. As far as just pulling, trying to make the dogs go faster, he was better than any of them. He would actually look back at the rest of the dogs when he was pulling, when he was working as hard as he could, and it would be as if he was saying, 'Is that the best you guys can do?'"

Lingo now relaxes in the yard, enjoying his retirement.

"He is aware he's somebody special," said Attla. "He acts like he owns the yard, like he's the boss."

Lingo's attitude of authority makes Attla laugh. In the equivalent of human years, Lingo is more than a hundred and showing signs of his age. The retired leader moves slower than he used to, even when preening in front of the other dogs, and he falls sick often. Attla figures Lingo is using up his retirement fund in trips to the veterinarian. In 1991 alone, Lingo cost a thousand dollars in medical bills. "But he's the father of a lot of good dogs in the lot," Attla said.

You can't blame Lingo for thinking he's king of the lot. After all, no other dog sat to have his portrait painted.

Chapter 22

World Titles

By 1976, when Attla won his second consecutive world championship, Lombard was fading from the picture. He remained a regular racer, even a challenger, but his period of dominance was over.

That year, Alfred Attla, George's younger brother by eight years, had his own dog team in its prime and also entered the world championship. He had Trot, who would become one of Attla's best leaders ever, in front, and he finished third. Just for a moment, George wondered whether his own brother would catch him, especially after Alfred won the first day's heat by eight seconds.

"I had a lot of confidence I'd beat him after the first day," said George. "That night I had to take care of some of his dogs, patch their feet. I was giving him a bad time about not being able to keep out of my way, and I was telling him I was going to beat him.

"The next day, before the race, I picked up Freckles, my leader, carried her over to Alfred's truck and held her up showing him her rear end. I said, 'You better have a good look because this is all you're going to see today.' I caught him that day."

If you're going to race your brother, you've got to psyche your brother. Donna Gentry surprised George and won that heat, though, and took the third day's heat, too. But Attla won the race with the best elapsed time without ever winning a heat.

Carl Huntington won his second Fur Rendezvous in 1977, in an abbreviated, two-day race, with Attla falling behind by three minutes on the first day and running out of time to mount a comeback. "There was a lot of ice and it got really warm," said Attla.

The trail turned into an impossible obstacle course for the dogs. If they had tried to run, they would have suffered serious foot injuries, sleds would have been tossed on their sides, and mushers would have been injured, too. Officials cut the race short for safety.

Attla was irritated because Huntington leased Trot from Alfred. George had been counting on leasing Trot that winter, and one day he got a phone call from Alfred saying he had a good offer from Huntington.

"He called me up and said, 'I can get fifteen hundred dollars rent for this dog. Do you want to pay that much?'" said George. "I said, 'No, that's too much money.' Carl leased it and won the Rendezvous."

In response, after the race, Attla bought Trot from Alfred for twenty-five hundred dollars, and the dog became a key leader in the team that emerged as one of his best.

"That was a lot of rent money," said Attla.

The loss in 1977 proved to be an interruption. Approaching the age of forty-five, when most athletes are well past their prime and starting to get cozy in retirement, Attla was beginning to reap the long-term rewards from the establishment of his kennel.

Trot and Keys were the leaders as Attla captured victory after victory in his pursuit of Lombard's record. Attla reclaimed the world championship in 1978, absolutely crushing the field. He won the first day's heat by less than a minute, but his dogs got faster and faster as everyone else's tired over the next two days. Attla won the race by seven minutes over second-place finisher Joee Redington.

Lombard was fifth that year, and in 1979, Attla was again champion with Lombard falling to sixth place. Second-place finisher, Andy Klingbell, was more than five minutes behind Attla. He was trouncing everyone.

The victory in 1979 was a milestone for George. He had been chasing Lombard for so long, and now he had finally caught him. It was George's eighth world title, and that put him even with Lombard. One more win and he could start thinking about his legacy of being known as the greatest dog musher of all time.

The peculiar race conditions of 1977 were repeated in 1980. Once again, slick, dangerous, icy trail confronted the mushers, and the race was chopped to two days. Dick Brunk was the champion, and Attla finished fourth.

New faces were popping up in the races all the time. Harris Dunlap, an eventual champion, came from upstate New York. Raymie Redington, another son of Joe Redington, Sr., the founder of the Iditarod, tried sprint mushing. Gareth Wright's daughter, then named Roxy Woods, an eight-time winner of the women's world championship, moved into the open class to go head-to-head with the men, and she finished third in 1980.

There was one constant, though. If you held a sprint mushing race, you could count on George Attla's being in it. And if George Attla was in a race, you could also count on his being at or near the front.

In 1981, Attla was racing for more than just a single title. He was racing for his place in history. Lombard was entered, but it was clear he was not the chief competition anymore. He ended up scratching from that race. It was a race that packed more adventure and drama into the twenty-five-mile loop than just about any other.

Lombard was not the only musher who didn't finish that year. Earl Norris didn't make it, and neither did Dunlap nor Manfred Malkema.

"What happened was that there was a tree in the trail just where we went around a turn," Attla recalls. "I made a left-hand turn, and there was a tree in the way as I swung the sled out. It was hard to miss that tree. Lombard hit that tree and lost his dogs, and he scratched. So did the others.

"I hit that tree, too. I hit it with my sled, and it was right where my bad leg was planted. The sled runners hit my feet, and I thought I'd broken them. I made it around the track, but boy, it hurt. Right after the first heat, I went to the hospital for X-rays. Nothing was broken, but I tell you my feet were swollen and blue."

Charlie Champaine, who would later marry Roxy Woods and combine their teams into an unbeatable kennel, had been on the rise in recent years. A tall man with a thick, walrus mustache, Champaine cut an imposing figure. He first sampled the Rendezvous in 1978 and finished tenth. In 1980, he finished sixth, and on the first day of the 1981 race, he won the heat, finishing four minutes ahead of Attla.

There was no way Attla could know he was going head-to-head with the future that day, with the man who, in partnership with Roxy, would emerge as his next great rival.

At the races, big and small, Attla commands attention. The fans know him and surround his dog truck when he is parked at Tudor Track at Anchorage. For the big races downtown, they lean over the fencing to watch as he hooks up his dogs. He is an institution in the state, so even the other mushers steal looks at him as he readies for a race.

When she was first starting out, Janet Clarke was mesmerized by Attla. She said she had to remind herself to ready her own team and not study Attla's moves.

"He has so much character," she said, "it strikes you right away. Even at the race track, eyes just follow him around."

Champaine said that when he was introduced to Attla at the North American in 1978, he was in awe. A little later, after he raced well, Champaine said he approached Attla about buying a dog. Attla remembered him. But when Champaine inquired about buying the dog, he was turned down. "Attla said, 'Nope. Too close first try. Sorry,'" said Champaine. "I didn't know what to say."

At that point in his career, Champaine considered it an honor just to race against Attla. He was hoping some day he'd somehow beat him. "For a novice," said Champaine, "the first time you beat George Attla, even for a day, there's something special about that. It means you've arrived. He commands a different level of respect than anyone else. It's kind of an exciting feeling. Even if you just win a heat."

By 1981, Champaine was coming on strong even without George's assistance.

Attla humbled the field on the second day, winning the heat by two minutes over his old friend, Marvin Kokrine, and by five minutes over Champaine.

"I had a way superior dog team," said Attla, "but I was in-between leaders that year. I didn't have a really good leader, and I had problems during the race. The time they were capable of running didn't really show up. The real problems began right away on the third day."

Keys was one of the leaders, but he certainly wasn't having a good day, and Attla had no other dog to step in. The dogs were out of control, spooked by the big crowds. Instead of sticking to the main route on Fourth Avenue, they dashed down a side street. Attla couldn't stop them, and they cut over the pavement, off the snow, to the plowed roads. They ran like that for a full block before he was able to steer them back to the trail. The snow layer was so thin he couldn't put the snow hook in, leaving him at the mercy of the dogs.

The dogs ran around the block, finally got straightened out, and rejoined the trail just as Champaine was mushing along. The two teams collided, creating a big mess. Bystanders helped separate the teams, but barely a half-mile into the race Champaine, who started second, had caught Attla.

This was one day when the dogs were letting Attla know who was boss. He finally made it down Cordova Hill onto the trail leading out of downtown Anchorage. They picked up speed, but then cut off the trail, down a slough near Mulcahy Stadium, the big Anchorage baseball park, and then along came Harvey Drake, another racer, passing from behind.

As he passed above Attla on the right trail, Drake yelled, "It's a beautiful day, isn't it, George?"

Attla was steamed. It was not a beautiful day in his neighborhood. He was almost ready to quit the race because he thought the leaders would never run. He tried a new dog called Prune in lead, and somehow Prune changed the chemistry of the team. The dogs took off at a gallop—this time on the trail. A short distance later, Attla approached Drake, but still bristling from Drake's teasing remark, Attla wanted to make a point. Instead of calling "Trail!" to ensure there would be no tangles, he zipped by in one push.

"My dogs ran right by his when they were still running," said Attla. "I thought about saying, 'Beautiful day, isn't it, Harvey?' But I didn't. We were just flying. I was concentrating on catching Charlie."

Some time passed before Attla saw Champaine on the course. He was moving swiftly, his dog team a synchronized machine, eating up ground. But Attla's dogs were real thoroughbreds. Now that they had their minds on the task, they were making up the lost time. Attla passed Champaine, took the lead, and held it, though he didn't lose Champaine.

After looping through the woods and coming towards the Tudor Track, which is the course for races held in the weeks leading up to the Fur Rendezvous, Attla's dogs got confused again. Instead of following the trail leading back to downtown and the finish line, they decided this race must also end at Tudor Track, a familiar territory.

"We were near the Tudor Track finishing chute," said Attla, "and my dogs knew the chute was right there, since that's where they'd been finishing all year. We were going at a good clip, but when they came to the low brush near the track, the low trees, they made a leap and went right over the trees. It happened so fast I didn't have a chance to stop them. We bounced into a landing. But the crazy thing is, Charlie followed me."

Attla's dogs had their tug lines tied in knots from their jump, and it took valuable time for George to turn the team around and point them in the right direction. Champaine had a smoother landing.

Champaine was in a position to pass and make the charge to the finish, just a few miles away, but when Attla got back on the trail and stopped in the middle of it, he put his snow hook in the ground, turned back and yelled, "Hey, wait a minute, Charlie!" Champaine stopped and waited.

"Charlie was pretty much a beginner back then," said Attla. "He waited. He had the right to pass me, and I think if he had passed me, he would have won the race. He was young. By agreeing to wait, Charlie gave me the race."

Attla lost the day's heat, but won the race by twenty seconds for his record-breaking ninth world championship. The twenty seconds likely could have been made up by Champaine.

Years later, reflecting on his mistake, Champaine said he was just overwhelmed by the mystique of George Attla, so when Attla told him to wait, he listened and waited. He didn't think about what he'd done until later.

"I was so new and so awed by the might of George Attla," said Champaine. "I was not mentally prepared to win. It was less than an aggressive and confident posture on my part. I just assumed George Attla would beat me. He did con me. He beat me on that and on experience. I never let it happen again. I learned from the master that time."

Champaine learned well. He won his first world championship in 1984 and won again in 1988, 1990, and 1991. When he retired after the 1991 season, his four titles placed him third on the all-time list behind Attla and Doc Lombard. Roxy Wright Champaine, Charlie's wife at the time, became the first woman to win an open world championship in 1989. The duo emerged as the dominant kennel in the sport and maintained that position until Roxy retired in 1996 with three open world titles, three North American titles, and nine women's world championships on her resume.

Attla was jovial at the finish line after pulling off his scam and notching another world championship. But he couldn't let the occasion pass without tweaking Drake. When Drake finished fourth, his clothes dripping wet with sweat, Attla was there to greet him. "I said, 'Hey, beautiful day, isn't it, Harvey?'" said Attla. "I just had to get my last little bit in."

A year later, in still another race cut short because of weather conditions, Attla won his tenth world title. He won the first heat by eleven seconds over Clyde Mayo, but built a three-minute lead by the end of the second day. It was the condensed version of the Rondy, but the world title still counted.

Attla was nearly fifty years old, but he was still a tough old dude. The years ahead promised more of the same. There would be many more world championships. Lombard didn't race in 1982, and he scratched in 1983. More than seventy years old, he made his final world championship appearance in the 1984 Rondy, finishing sixteenth.

The path was clear now. Attla was king, and he planned to keep control of his kingdom.

Chapter 23

Spirit of the Wind

The big, black limousine cruised along the jammed roads adjacent to the beaches of the French Riviera. Lashed to the roof of the limo was a dog sled.

Inside sat George Attla, the man whose first, last, and best mode of transportation had always been the dog sled. It was hot, it was sunny, the people were bizarre, and it was a total blast.

This came under the heading of, "Pinch me, I must be dreaming." One day in the late Seventies, Attla picked up his mail and found a letter from two strangers making an interesting proposal. John Logue and Ralph Liddle, at the time independent filmmakers based in Juneau, wrote to Attla and told him they'd like to make a movie about his life. They had been inspired by an article they read about him in *Reader's Digest* some time before.

And that was how, in 1980, Attla, world-champion dog musher, came to be the most curious of tourists at the Cannes Film Festival.

"There really was never very much money involved," he said. "These two guys didn't have any money. They were just interested in doing a story, and it was really fascinating to me that they got the backing and were able to do it."

The movie, made by Windham Hill Films, focused on Attla's village years and his turn to dog mushing. It was released as *Spirit of the Wind* and it carried that title when it received rave reviews and won Best Picture at the U.S. Film Festival. It also won the Silver Halo Award from the Motion Picture Council, the Best Picture designation and several other awards at the American Indian Film Festival, and a special Humanism in Cinema Award at the Moscow Film Festival. In addition—and this was how Attla came to be in France—it was chosen to represent the U.S. at the Cannes International Film Festival.

Attla signed a contract with the initiators of the project, and they visited him at his fish camp on the Yukon River during the summer. They interviewed him about his life, and while there, they helped him with his fishing. Liddie and Logue wrote the screenplay in the fish camp, and the project was financed by Doyon, the Native corporation based in Fairbanks.

The movie went into production quickly, and filming began that winter in Ely, Minnesota, of all places, while Attla was making the circuit of the Midwestern races.

At first, Attla stayed close to the filmmakers. He thought the whole thing was kind of neat, people wanting to make a movie about him. But the movie makers were on a tight budget, there was no way to look at the film day by day. Attla got a little bored.

"At the end of the day you had nothing," he said. "You can't see what you've got right away. It was like you couldn't see what you got for the money. You can't see the accomplishment, so I lost interest in the whole process."

The whole process went on around Attla, but he also had races to run, dogs to raise and train.

The selection process of dogs for the movie was fairly humorous. The movie telescoped many years of Attla's life, and it didn't matter to the filmmakers which dog was a leader at which time in his actual racing career. The search for dogs who responded well to commands and who were photogenic involved trying out several dogs from the yard and even experimenting with dogs belonging to others.

At one point, said Attla, a dog trained for certain commands by Mary Shields, the first woman to complete the Iditarod, was used. But the dog didn't work out. Attla left his son Gary in charge of the dogs for the filmmakers. Gary made sure they were treated right and supplied the ones needed for most scenes. For the most part, they turned out to be dogs that were still active, still in their racing prime. In the movie, the leader of Attla's racing team is called Jarvy, but the dog was actually played by Trot, one of his best leaders in real life.

"It takes a certain kind of dog to act and do those things, I guess," said Attla. "They would take a shot and it wasn't right, so they had to shoot it over again. Some scenes they'd have to shoot over and over. And it takes a certain kind of dog to stick with that.

"After a while, some of the dogs would say, 'The heck with it; this is no fun.' They'd get dragged back to the starting line, or wherever, and be forced to start again. They'd get tired of that. They don't like it. Trot, though, had the right kind of personality for it. Everything was fun for her. She was just a friendly dog. You could bring her in the house."

Trot was the star dog in the show. The dog Shields trained was supposed to be the star, said Attla, because it looked the part of a tough husky, but Attla didn't think it had the right personality. "They tried to make a movie actor out of him, and it didn't work."

The movie, an hour and forty minutes long, traced Attla's early life in the Bush when he first discovers he has tuberculosis, through his difficult adjustment in the hospital, his struggles early in his mushing career, then through the inspirational and stunning victory in the world championship in 1958.

The musical soundtrack includes original tunes by Buffy Sainte-Marie, features actors Chief Dan George and Slim Pickens, and introduces newcomer Pius Savage of Anchorage as the adult Attla. More recently, Savage acted in *White Fang*, another Alaska-based film. George's mother is played by his older sister, Rose Ambrose.

It is a pleasant, low-key performance, with Attla's mother being shown as a caring woman with an abundance of common sense and wisdom. Ambrose had a good time being in the movies, and she thought the picture was accurate in its portrayal of George's life.

"It was interesting for me to do," she said, "and I like it. It showed us in the old days and showed the family ways and the village. It was exciting for me to play my mother. I was proud to do that for my mom."

Attla was satisfied with the final product, though it was a strange sensation watching someone else portraying him and watching his own life story being written and illustrated by others. Attla thought Savage did a good job and that, overall, the movie was fair and enjoyable. "It was very accurate," he said. "They didn't alter anything." Growing up in Huslia, with a different cultural background, and only being exposed to movies and television at an older age, Attla had a different view of the big and small screens than children who sit in front of TVs for hours at a time. For those kids, make-believe coming to their neighborhood would be the thrill of a lifetime. Attla had a slightly more pragmatic view of the world. "I never was impressed by movie actors or actresses," said Attla, "because what they do isn't real. It's pretend. To me it never seems real. I thought Pius Savage did a good job. I did give him some advice, but mostly I stayed away from the filming."

There was no filming in Huslia, but the filmmakers used other Alaska villages, Rampart and Porcupine, and George helped set up the producers in their own fish camp near the Yukon Bridge he helped build so many years before. The fishing scenes were shot at that camp. Some of Attla's children had minor parts, too.

When the filming began, Attla followed the work intently, but that didn't last. "I don't think it took me more than a couple of days to say, 'This is not my line of work,'" he said.

The filming was spread over all four seasons, so it took about a year to complete. The movie has become a classic in Alaska, and it is sometimes shown in auditoriums in Anchorage during the Fur Rendezvous celebration or in Fairbanks to coincide with the North

American. It was featured on *Showtime,* though it was never shown in theatres in general release. Many Alaska mushers taped the movie when it showed on TV, and they watch it frequently.

Janet Clarke is one of them. She said she watches *Spirit of the Wind* all the time for inspiration, and one of the strangest sensations she had was watching the movie, then going out to a race soon after to compete against Attla. It was a slightly disorienting experience, she said.

"The movie didn't make him any more of a hero than he seemed like in person," said Clarke. "I remember thinking that, in person, he was just as legendary. It was an odd feeling to be at the track and seeing him and thinking, 'I just watched a movie of this guy's life.' One of the things you have to get over is that he's still one of the competitors. You have to believe you can beat him before you can. It took a little bit of time." That was bonus psyching for Attla.

As a youth, Attla never ventured farther from Huslia than fish camp. Then, when he got sick, he had treatment in other parts of Alaska. He was nearly forty years old when he left the state for the first time, but he discovered during his tours of the Midwest that he enjoyed visiting other areas. He was thrilled when the film opened new avenues for travel.

Before going to France, Attla went on tour with the movie, making appearances in San Francisco, Washington, D.C., and Tacoma, Washington, among other places. He was introducing Athabascan culture to whites in the Lower 48 with his story, and he was introducing the sport of dog mushing to people whose only knowledge of huskies came from reading Jack London tales. First, the movie would be shown to the audience. It opens with a statement that the movie's beginning is set in Huslia in the 1930s. Then Attla was introduced to speak.

"A lot of them were surprised I was still alive," he said. "It was pretty funny. That was my first reaction to these people, that they went, 'Wow, this guy's still alive.'"

The film's publicity touted *Spirit of the Wind,* or *Attla,* as the picture was later re-titled, as "a motion picture whose greatest appeal is its humanity. It is also that rare bird: a feel-good film whose pleasure at viewing is not just momentary. The characters you meet in *Attla* have the honesty, humor, and authenticity to be friends and memories for life."

The movie was very well-received by the critics. There was much glowing praise from major newspapers when the movie was unveiled in the United States.

The Los Angeles Times wrote: "*Attla* is a rousing, warm-hearted adventure with spirit and authenticity. It is touching, invigorating, exquisitely photographed, a real banquet for the eye."

"*Attla* celebrates the human spirit. It is uplifting and inspirational. We hear the ominous crack and groan of ice on the Yukon River and we are in the country of Jack London." That was a comment in *The San Francisco Examiner.*

"A stunning film. There is gorgeous cinematography, wonderful acting, a haunting musical score. It captures the heart." That was part of the analysis in *The New York Post.*

Spirit of the Wind does a good job of summarizing Attla's angst upon returning to the village after his hospitalization. It does a superb job of depicting a young man torn between two cultures, who has trouble fitting in with the old lifestyle of his people.

"That was true," said Attla. "Missing my growing up period was hard, and the movie did a good job with that. They were accurate in what they showed. That was a painful period, and after I started dog racing, I did become my own person. They showed that. What they showed was generally true. It wasn't literally true, but it was right."

There were scenes in the movie that showed Attla as a disturbed young man who drowned some of his sorrows by drinking, and Attla said that isn't exactly the case. He did drink a lot when he was younger, when the booze was available, but mostly at parties, and all through adulthood he enjoyed taking a drink, though not to forget his problems.

"All the drinking I did, I never lost a job because of it. If I partied and I had to go to work at eight in the morning, I went to work at eight in the morning," he said. "With a headache, but I went. But you can do that when you're young, you know. I can party all night. I can go to a banquet and party all night, but in the morning I get out there and take the dogs out of the truck. I've always been able to do that."

Once he reached his mid-fifties, though, Attla felt drinking and partying were harming his ability to race at his best. He went to one wedding reception, partied all night, and when he couldn't get out of bed to tend to his dogs, he decided it was time to give it up. So he gave up drinking altogether in the late Eighties.

"I got so damned sick from it, it wasn't worth it," he said. "I had headaches and hangovers, and I just stopped drinking. Maybe I'm just not as young as I used to be."

Attla had a lot of fun with the movie. There is a movie poster mounted on the wall in his kitchen, and although he doesn't own a copy, he has seen the movie about half a dozen times. It never has been released on video, though, so borrowing copies made by friends is the best way to come by it.

No part of the entire adventure thrilled Attla more than the trip to France, though. Attla and the filmmakers rented the limousine and placed the dog sled on top. Then they tied a moose horn on top of the sled and drove around town advertising the movie.

"It was quite a sight, I guess," said Attla. "We were a mobile exhibit for our film. We drove around, and people came up to us and asked us what it was all about. It was really crazy."

Attla just dug the entire scene. Mobs of trendily dressed tourists in their printed shirts and fancy sunglasses. Rocks on some beaches instead of sand. Pretty women sunbathing topless—with men walking right up to them and snapping their pictures.

"I thought that was funny as hell," said Attla, "I'll tell you one thing. It was nothing like Huslia."

Chapter 24

Retirement?

George Attla sat behind the wheel of his broken-down truck. The dogs howled, sending up a cacophony of sound that was a bonus irritant.

This was not the first breakdown. Attla was stuck on the Alaska Highway. He was returning from competing in the sprint dog circuit in the Lower 48, and this time he'd driven as far east as Saranac Lake, New York, the tiny community outside Lake Placid. Have dogs, will travel.

The transmission went out in Fort St. John, British Columbia, and he'd paid out some of his prize winnings to fix it. Several hundred miles up the road, the transmission bonked out again. He was stuck in Watson Lake in the Yukon Territory.

And the Fur Rondy started in a few days. Attla had to be in Anchorage for the world championships. This was one year he knew he had the best team. In his mind, there would be no repeat of Dick Brunk's two-day, truncated victory of 1980. This race belonged to Attla. He knew it. All he had to do was get to it.

During Attla's streak of dominance in the late Seventies and early Eighties, people figured he would win as long as he showed up. Well, the 1981 race was one time he almost didn't show up.

The weakling transmission almost knocked Attla out of the race entirely. There was no transmission for sale in Watson Lake, and Attla had to have one shipped in from Fairbanks. George and his second wife, Karen, were invited to stay with the family of a Canadian Mounted Police officer. It was during an extreme cold snap, and the Attlas spent close to a week in the town. George ran out of dog food and started feeding his team commercial dog food off the local shelves.

The new transmission finally arrived, and the car was fixed. The Attlas quietly left town at four o'clock in the morning, trying to make time on the deserted road.

Only a mistake was made in the repairs. An extra piece of metal was welded into the wrong area, and a gasket burned out. Twelve miles down the road, the engine seized up again, and the truck had to be towed back to Watson Lake.

By this time, Attla was panicking. He had to get to Anchorage. "They took the truck back to the garage and broke it open," said Attla. "There was an oil leak. They could fix it up so it would run, but it didn't look like it would last very long."

But he couldn't wait for any more replacement parts to be shipped in. He had to go. Attla bought a case of transmission fluid and set out for Whitehorse, about three hundred miles to the north. After a half hour, the transmission was a quart low. About every fifteen minutes, it seemed, he had to stop the truck and add another quart. "Boy, I tell you that transmission smelled horrible and sounded terrible by the time we got to Whitehorse," he said.

When he got to Whitehorse, he went to the Ford dealership looking for another transmission. There was none to be had, but he told the owner his urgent reason to move on, so the man took a transmission out of a new vehicle and put it in the truck.

"Anyway, that took all my winnings that I'd won all winter," said Attla. "And it was two days before the start of the Rendezvous by the time they had the transmission installed."

Unfortunately, Attla had to go to North Pole to get more of his dog food before he could go to Anchorage.

"When we got to Anchorage, it was about seven o'clock at night the day before the first heat," he said. "I could see the morning of the race how tired the dogs were, and when I took them out of the truck, they weren't that happy. They had been lying around too much, and they hadn't been eating properly. I was pretty tired, too."

Attla finished fourth on the first day, but then rallied with his recovering team to best Charlie Champaine in their close, controversial race.

"The next day, when I took the dogs out of the truck in the morning, you could see they were feeling much better," said Attla. "I had a fantastic dog team. They shouldn't have been fourth that first day, but it was all that riding in the truck. Boy, they sure bounced back well. Those dogs did fantastic things."

This was a period of time when Attla dogs were the best, and after he won the world championship again in 1982, his tenth victory, there was no reason to think he wouldn't reign for a long time.

But although he wasn't talking about it much, Attla was starting to feel old. His main competitors were the children of his first rivals. A second generation was coming up, and here was good old George, still going, still winning.

Who was he racing against in the Eighties? Roxy Wright-Champaine, daughter of Gareth. Chuck and Curtis Erhart, sons of Lester Erhart. Lester was a close friend for years who often loaned dogs to Attla. Attla teased him. "You call me a friend all these years, and here you are sending your sons in to whip my ass," Attla told him.

And, of course, Attla could see Lombard fading as a threat. In the early Eighties, Doc Lombard was starting to grow frail.

"I could see his health was gone," said Attla. "He was weaker. He was having trouble putting the dogs in the dog box. That kind of stuff. His physical strength was going, and he had Alzheimer's disease. It was starting. He had all kinds of problems, though you could tell he was still enjoying what he was doing.

"I could see it was over for him. There's always a lot of people who say that Lombard should have quit when he was on top. But he was doing what he enjoyed. If a person enjoys what he's doing, he's there for the right reasons. He loved his dogs. He loved taking care of his dogs. You can't say that a guy should quit when he's on top. He still liked it."

Attla could see time passing Lombard by, and a new, frisky group of challengers was on its way up.

Attla finished third in the 1983 Rendezvous. Harris Dunlap won; Attla was nine minutes behind him. Champaine beat Attla in the Rondy for the first time, placing second. And in 1984, Champaine won his first crown, and Attla had his worst race ever, finishing thirteenth after suffering with the problem with his finger. Also by 1984, Attla hadn't won the North American in five years.

In the late Seventies, Tesoro, the oil and gas company, signed on as Attla's chief sponsor. The company provided the food for his dogs and covered his expenses. Feeling on the old side as he passed fifty, and feeling on the down side after his poor race, Attla told Wade Rogers, his contact at Tesoro, that he was thinking of retiring.

"I didn't have many good dogs at the time, and I actually thought about quitting," said Attla. "It seemed like it might be a good time. I had to rebuild the team, and I really wasn't that interested."

There are no football players in their fifties—Hall of Fame quarterback George Blanda stayed in the game until he was in his late forties. There are no baseball players in their fifties—Hall of Fame pitcher Nolan Ryan came pretty close. In the entire annals of American sport, there have been few serious competitors of that age as Attla was in 1984. Jockey Billy Shoemaker is one, and hockey player Gordie Howe is another, but the examples aren't plentiful.

When an athlete ages, he hears the whispers. The legs go first, people say. The eyes go first, others say. In the case of George Attla, of course, those are humorous observations. His legs went before he even started. His eyes went bad when he was in his prime. As usual, Attla defied normal convention.

There were many friends and advisors who suggested gently for the first time that Attla consider retirement. At the moment, he was receptive to such suggestions.

"In George's case, it's definitely true that he needs something to motivate himself," said Jim Welch. "The longer he goes, the more he needs something special to keep going. Sometimes just getting angry at the competition has been enough. Sometimes it's been just getting angry at himself."

The same Attla who put off a buyer for Lingo around this same time by asking for an astronomical sum, told Rogers there was no way he would continue racing unless he got a ten-thousand-dollar increase in his sponsorship.

"I thought he would say no," said Attla. "And he said, I'll get back to you next week.'"

When Rogers called back, he told George he had to race and that Tesoro would give him the money. Responding to that vote of confidence, Attla went on a dog-buying spree. He bought close to forty dogs, but only one special one, Spotty, the same dog he later sold to Janet Clarke as a reliable leader.

So Attla once again prepared himself to race. However, in the short period between 1982 and 1984, he had gone from seemingly invincible on the starting line to an old man in the eyes of some racers. Certainly he was old, but the question was whether he was over the hill.

Attla, the ultimate competitor, had an attitude as flat as day-old soda. The man who refused to race for second didn't seem to be hungry enough to race for first in the mid-Eighties. He still flirted with the idea of retirement.

What else was there for him to do? He had won a record ten world championships. He had won championships in four different decades. He had won six North American titles. Doc Lombard was retired. Gareth Wright wasn't racing all the time. The new group of mushers were all young enough to be his children. The spark was missing.

"It was a mentally down period," said Attla. "But one of the things that went through my mind about quitting was that I didn't know what I would do with myself. I constantly asked myself, 'What will I do?' There were some things I wanted to do in my life that I couldn't do because of my leg. I wanted to be a heavy equipment operator, but I couldn't do that. I did run a machine once in a mining camp, but I was no good at it.

"I really didn't have anything that would be better. That was the problem. I'd always been happy with what I was doing. Even now, years later, just going out the door this morning to water my dogs, they were happy to see me. It's a good feeling when they jump up and bark when they see me. They're really happy that I'm out there. I got all these animals, and they're happy to see me, they're glad I'm there.

"There's lulls in any competitive sport," he said.

In a career that spans thirty-five years, it is hard to stay focused one hundred percent of the time. Concentration and commitment are demanded to reach and stay at the top. For a few years Attla wondered if he really cared about being the best anymore. He had proven it already, hadn't he? Should he retire? Should he rebuild? He was having a crisis.

Attla decided to stick with racing for a little while longer. He would try to make the necessary sacrifices, put in the time, work at the same all-out speed to become a champion again. Only he would alter his strategy a little. If the mushers were all going to think of him as an old man, he'd let them think that way.

In his own mind, Attla was still the king. But the man who always looked for an edge thought he may have found another one. Let them all think he was burned out. Maybe he'd catch them off guard.

The musher who first recognized Attla's approach, and who best appreciated it, was another veteran. Gareth Wright figured out what Attla was doing.

"I think he set up a situation where he didn't put too much pressure on himself," said Wright. "People were saying, 'Poor George Attla.' He thought he could sneak up on people. And maybe he could sneak up on them in that way. It's a strategy a wise, older person would use, not a young, boisterous person."

Now Attla could play the part of an elder statesman. But if mushers thought he would be content in that simpler role behind the winner, they were very wrong. He would wait for his turn, and he would show the youngsters what racing was all about.

Fast Eddy Streeper, a brash upstart from Fort Nelson, British Columbia, provided what many thought Attla would never again find: motivation.

Chapter 25

Huslia Hustler

Fast Eddy blew everyone away in 1985. Really blew everyone away.

He was the fast gun who came to town boasting, and then proved himself by mowing down everyone else who used to think they were fast. That year, Streeper, just twenty-five years old, won the world championship easily. He built a five-minute lead on the first day and coasted home first by fourteen minutes. Second place went to Jim Harvey, Charlie Champaine scratched, and Attla finished sixth, although his second-day time was second-best overall.

"I was thinking about retirement until Eddy came along," said Attla. "That was the best thing that could have happened to me. He got me mad, but I really needed that."

Fast Eddy got a lot of people mad, not just Attla, when he announced to an *Anchorage Daily News* reporter that legendary George Attla, ten-time world champion George Attla, was over the hill, washed up, and should retire.

"His day is done," Streeper announced. "He doesn't have the dogs anymore. He's done it wrong somewhere along the line."

There was quite an uproar after Streeper said that. Folks didn't take well to having a newcomer talk so harshly.

Gareth Wright was one who came to Attla's defense immediately. "What makes George Attla great," he said at the time, "is what made General Eisenhower great, or Kennedy great. He was born great."

Of course, Attla bristled about the comments. Did Attla need renewed inspiration? Yes. And Streeper provided it.

Streeper did indeed have the best dog team in 1985. There was no disputing that. He went on to win the North American a month later, too. But his words had stung Attla. In the Athabascan culture, elders demand respect. People who have recorded great achievements demand respect. By this time, at age fifty-one, Attla fit both descriptions.

It was one thing to consider retirement on his own terms. It was quite another to have a bragging stranger try to push him out of the sport he loved. Attla never confronted Streeper about the comments in the paper; he filed them away in his own mind and used them as a spur. Eddy knew what he had said. Attla knew what Eddy had said. That was enough. The rest was up to George: it was time to take care of business again.

"I don't think Eddy himself realized how much he had helped me," said Attla. "I don't think I would have come back as fast if he didn't say that, or had the desire to. I think he should have shown me more respect.

"I did my thing with my life. If a person does what he wants to do in his lifetime and had a lot of success at it, I don't think anybody should come along and say the guy's washed up. I don't think anybody has the right to say that. I've proven I can do the job, you know. He actually hurt my feelings, that's what he did."

Streeper's insult—and Attla took it that way—gave him a goal when he thought he had no more to pursue. It also reminded him how much he enjoyed dog mushing, and how he wanted to stick with it as long as he could.

"That's his life," said Charlie Champaine. "That's his entire life. He has to do it for himself, and he does love it."

Jim Welch remembers Eddy Streeper's boasts about how he would break all the records, and he scoffs at them. The records belong to Attla and always will, Welch thinks. "He has a record that will never be matched," said Welch. "Eddy Streeper said he would set records. But I don't think anyone will win ten world championships again. It's not just a matter of skill, it's also persistence. It's easy to stay with things when you're at the top, but when things aren't rosy, it's harder."

A month after Streeper proclaimed Attla over the hill, Attla finished second behind him at the North American. "That wasn't too bad for an old guy that was washed up, was it?" asked Attla. "I knew in my own mind that I was going to beat him. I had some young leaders, and I'd been around dogs long enough to know that sometimes they age fast. You might win the world championship one year, and you might feel like you've got a super dog team, but dogs get old fast. It had happened to me enough times, hadn't it? I knew my dogs would get better. I knew I was going to get Eddy eventually."

Attla always said the only time he was patient was around dogs. That included dog races. If he could wait four years between 1958 and 1962 to rebuild his dog team for a second run at the Fur Rendezvous, he could bide his time for Eddy Streeper.

George wanted Streeper in 1986, but he kept his own counsel, making no predictions. And it was just as well, because for the first time ever, there was no snow in Anchorage for the race. There had been a handful of occasions when the course turned so icy it was dangerous to run, and the race had been shortened to two heats. But the snowless trail was impossible to run on. It was the only time the Rondy was cancelled.

However, Streeper did travel north for the North American. More than a year had passed since he suggested Attla was washed up, but no one had forgotten the remark. Leading up to the race, news organizations quoted the statement repeatedly, reminded everyone just what kind of bad blood there might be between the two contenders.

Streeper was given the opportunity to retract, to apologize, to say that he didn't really mean it, but he did not do so. Instead, he emphasized his feelings; George was still washed up in his mind.

"I think he got egged on a lot," said Attla. "And he kept putting his foot in his mouth. He kept saying more. Some people were giving him the chance to take it back, but you can't take something like that back. It just got worse.

"I didn't have to say anything," said George. "Even the year before, when he said it, after the North American, we went to the Tok Race of Champions, and I beat him. It wasn't the world championship, but I caught him and passed him. But I didn't say anything at all. I kept a low profile."

Until the racing began in Fairbanks. With the elimination in Anchorage, the North American was the only big race of the season that year.

On the first day, Attla blazed over the twenty-mile course and set a new record. "I wanted to get him in the Rondy, but the Rondy was cancelled," said Attla. "When I beat him the first day in Fairbanks, I was egging him on, too. 'Not too bad for a washed up guy,' I said to the reporters."

Attla was getting his message across on the trail and in the press. He won the second day's heat and won the race, his seventh North American title. The smile of satisfaction after that championship could be seen from a mile away—on a cloudy day.

A year later, Streeper won his second world championship, and his closest competitor was Attla. George captured the third day's heat, but lost the race by one minute, twenty-six seconds. He was certainly letting Eddy know he was around.

In March 1987, Attla won the North American for an eighth time. Coupled with his ten Fur Rendezvous titles, that gave him eighteen major championships. He was back in business. He'd proven there was still some fight in the old man yet. If anyone else thought Fast Eddy was right, that Attla belonged on the sidelines as a cheerleader, they got educated in a hurry. All the mushers were once again looking over their shoulders for the Huslia Hustler.

Two weeks before the 1992 world championship race, Janet Clarke was discussing Attla. "He hasn't had a very good year, but watch, he'll storm it and win it," she said.

No one will ever make Eddy's mistake again, believes Attla's friend Rudy Demoski. "Before every race he's totally focused," he said. "He becomes tense and he really focuses in. He's very meticulous. Everything has to be down to the nitty-gritty. He has everything figured out days in advance, and he's all ready. That hasn't changed. Once he gets behind that sled, he's outwardly calm. He'll never lose his professionalism.

"In the back of everyone's mind, he's still the guy you've got to beat. It's a milestone for any musher when they beat him, and the first time they ever beat him, it's 'Wow, I just beat George Attla.' It's a feeling of, 'If I beat him, I beat somebody.' They're damned good if they do that, but they ain't the legend he is."

After Attla got his revenge by winning the 1986 North American, he was a happy guy. He never did talk to Streeper, or gloat in front of him, and he says Streeper never approached him either. Streeper still periodically comes back to Anchorage to race, but the two men have never had a conversation since Streeper claimed George was washed up. They've been in the same room for pre-race position drawings and post-race banquets, but they don't socialize.

"We keep out of each other's way," said Attla. "I think it bothers him that he said that. He was young and he made a mistake."

Attla likens Streeper's faux pas to his own rambunctious behavior when he acted wildly at his first big village race, and the older woman warned him that he would rue his actions later in life. And, he said, yes, it's true, that is how he feels now.

"It's not easy to live down what Eddy said because he got a lot of publicity," said Attla. "What Eddy said was completely wrong. It bothered me. And I think it bothered him a little bit once he said it, but instead of just letting it blow over, he kept saying things that didn't come out sounding right. I just did my thing."

For a few years, Streeper did his racing outside of Alaska, but he returned in the Nineties.

"I think he's a different Eddy, that he's grown up a lot," said Attla. "He doesn't owe me an apology. I don't think that. I got my shot back at him. I figure we're even. Let it go at that."

Chapter 26

Guile and Guts

The Eddy Streeper challenge rekindled the fire in George Attla. Although their little feud didn't prove that Attla was back in charge, it did mean he was a contender again, a threat. Anyone who forgot it would be taught a lesson. Go stand in the corner until your memory improves.

Attla responded to Streeper's comments by winning two straight North American titles, but when the glow from his retaliation began to fade, he once more slipped into a mental slump. He wasn't as down or confused as he had been before the revival, but he discovered that the old hunger and desire couldn't be sustained for every minute of every race.

George finished second in the 1988 world championship, more than five minutes behind Charlie Champaine. Streeper did not even race. This marked the beginnings of the new dynasty, the ascension of the Charlie Champaine-Roxy Wright-Champaine team.

"I think the good feeling of beating Eddy was burning out just a little bit," said Attla. "I had already proven my point. I wanted to prove that I wasn't washed up yet. I wanted to prove that in the worst way. And, at my age, I think I needed somebody to take a shot at me. It helped me get some of the desire back. People told me, 'I'm glad you beat that smart-aleck kid.'"

Athletes, like all individuals, evolve. In the beginning, their natural talents carry them. Then they become more aware of their sport, more learned. They acquire knowledge and apply it. As they slow down—and athletes in every sport slow down one way or another—they make up for the erosion of speed with expertise. Where once they won on reflexes and quickness, now they might win on guile and guts.

As they age, as well, athletes who were once single-minded may acquire other interests. These interests may be diversionary. This was all true of George Attla in the Eighties.

He was aging. There was no denying that. Also, he'd been at the top of his game and at the top of his sport for so long, it was inevitable that there would be some dulling of his fire. Over the years, one of his unique talents, though, had been an ability to focus. Now, however, for the first time he seemed to welcome distractions.

Attla split up with his second wife, Karen, in the early part of the decade. A few years later he met Tamara Ostlund, and their relationship blossomed in the late Eighties. George had two more kids with Tamara, who is more than thirty years younger than Attla. Frankie, who turned twelve in the summer of 2000, and Shaylin, who turned ten in the early fall of that year, are the youngest of his children.

"I think over most of my life I was too wound up with my dogs," said Attla. "I don't feel I gave enough time to my wives or to my kids. I've always had the dogs, and I was trying to win championships. These two kids have shown me what I've been missing in my life. They've shown me what I missed with my other kids."

From the time Frankie and Shaylin could toddle, Attla was an instructive father, shepherding them around the dog yard. Before he was five years old, Frankie would take visitors by the hand to the corner of the yard in order to show off the puppies. He grinned like a proud papa himself. As soon as she was old enough, Shaylin scampered through the yard, too.

"I used to run dogs all winter and work all summer on the river, or in fish camp," said Attla. "I'd be gone from April to October sometimes. These two little ones are showing me what I missed with my first family. It's just amazing how fast they're advancing."

Scraping for a living according to the seasons is a common experience in rural Alaska. If you are going to mush dogs in the winter and seek the biggest prizes in the sport, the task becomes an all-consuming one, and certainly a full-time one in the winter. If that means you must make most of your money in the summer, so be it. Often, though, that means going where the money is—away from home.

Steven Attla, said George, was a riverboat pilot for seventeen years, living his summers on the Yukon. His kids went to school at Mount Edgecumbe in search of a good education, so they were away from home half the year. Steven was away from home much of the other half when they were home.

"He told me just recently that he feels like he missed the whole part of their growing up," said George. "But it happens a lot in Alaska if you have to go away for summer work. I bet you most men are that way. Those are really critical years, those first four or five years for kids. They're growing so fast."

Tamara was a dog mushing fan in general, and a George Attla fan in particular, when she introduced herself at a race in 1986. She was only nineteen years old at the time, and neither of them could have predicted the ensuing romance.

"We've had a good time," said Attla. "It's amazing, maybe, that that's so with our age difference. But I never grew up. I tell her all the time, I never grew up. I don't want to grow up."

The joys of fatherhood interrupt Attla's thoughts constantly these days. He truly marvels at how his attitude about fatherhood has changed from when he was in his twenties. Perhaps because he genuinely feels he has nothing left to prove in racing, he can revel in a role he wasn't relaxed enough to deal with thirty years ago.

"People don't realize the time they're missing with their kids," he said, trying to spread his own wisdom to others who may not have seen the light. "I wouldn't have known this if I hadn't met Tamara and had two more kids. Do you realize I wouldn't have known what I had missed?"

Make no mistake, though, if Attla is more laid back, he is not merely stepping to the starting line of his races for the fun of it. When the race begins, Attla is a racer first.

Attla had two smart leaders, Moses and Grace, when he won the North American in 1986 and 1987, but he didn't have the depth in his team that he thought he needed to win the Fur Rendezvous.

"They were fast, but they weren't tough enough," said Attla. "Charlie and Roxy had the superior team. In 1988, Charlie was way superior. They were way superior to anything that's been on the track in the few years since then."

Charlie Champaine is tall and slender. He speaks quietly but eloquently, and he has a wry wit. Roxy, much shorter, is soft-spoken, and her natural inclination is to avoid the limelight.

As the Eighties turned to the Nineties, the stars at the front of the pack were changing once more. There were more mushers working their way up, putting in their time, and improving. Streeper had come and gone and come back again. His brother, Terry, chattier and perhaps less intense, came north to race. Greg Taylor was a new face on his way up. So was Janet Clarke. Curtis Erhart became a challenger. Curtis, in fact, is married to Shannon, another daughter of Gareth Wright, and though Gareth isn't racing his own dogs, he is now a coach.

"I'm training and breeding every day, and I'm trying to help them win a world championship," said Gareth. "If you've been a winner once, to me, there's something wrong with you if you keep going too long trying to win, especially if you've got a daughter who's a champion."

The new royalty in sprint mushing was the king, Charlie Champaine, and the queen, Roxy Wright-Champaine.

"Charlie is pretty similar to Roland Lombard," said Attla. "He's an easy-going person. You can't get him mad. Or at least I've never seen him mad. I try to psyche him out, and I work on Roxy, too. Both of them have put in a lot of time. I couldn't get them mad or psyched out. They don't let things bother them. Whatever you say or do doesn't seem to matter to them.

"I try to get to know my competitors, just like I did with Doc Lombard, what kind of people they are. I want to know what their weak points are as human beings. That helps to know. You have to know them probably as well as your own dogs."

What Attla learned was that the Champaines don't rattle. They come to the track with tough dogs, fast dogs, and they win with those dogs. Between 1988 and 1992, Charlie or Roxy won every world title. They also won three of four North American championships between 1989 and 1992.

Charlie announced his retirement from sprint mushing after the 1991 season in order to spend more time with his father and daughter, but Attla said he believes Champaine will be back some day. He really grew as a musher, according to Attla, after the 1981 race when Attla conned Champaine out of winning.

"He got more aggressive," said George. "Charlie became a good racer. In the early Eighties, Charlie had a pretty fair dog team, but I didn't think he was a good racer. He was conservative. He didn't go for broke. He always saved that little bit to make sure he got home.

"To me, I know that over the years there were times I could have run a better race if I was conservative, if I thought, 'Well, if I go this fast I'll hang on to fifth place.' Instead of doing that, I'd think, 'This is how fast my dogs have to go in order to win it.' I'd take the chance. And I finished lower 'cause the dogs gave out. There's not many racers who would do that."

George Attla doesn't race for second place.

In the 1989 world championship, Roxy bested George by two minutes, two seconds over the three days.

"That was one time, I think, she actually outran me," said Attla. "With her legs, she physically outran me on Cordova Hill. That was the area where she won each day. That was the place in there where I was losing it."

In 1988, after two straight wins in the North American, Attla was attempting to fulfill one of his longstanding goals by winning three straight—what Horace "Holy" Smoke had done between 1951 and 1953, and Doc Lombard between 1962 and 1964.

The competition came not from Charlie or Roxy, though, but from Marvin Kokrine. Kokrine, like Attla, lives in North Pole, though the family is originally from the village of Tanana. Kokrine is the son of Attla's old friend, Henry Kokrine. George had pretty much watched Marvin, who is twenty-two years younger, grow up.

"He was friends with my father, who used to loan him dogs," said Marvin. "When he came to town to race at the spring carnival, he stayed at the house."

Marvin was friends with Attla's oldest son, Gary, and at first really knew George only as a dog musher and as his father's pal. Marvin didn't aspire to become a dog musher, but his dad more or less forced the sport on him when he reached junior high school age. "My dad decided he wanted to make me a dog musher," said Marvin. "I imagine he thought it would keep me out of trouble."

When Marvin did show an interest in the sport, though, George took him under his wing. He gave him advice, tried to teach him the right way to do things, and pointed him in the right direction in training. This went on for years. When Henry, Marvin's father, died in the late Seventies, George commiserated with the entire family.

"He helped my mother out," said Marvin. "He helped us get back on our feet. Just by being there when the times were rough. He sure did help me, and he gave me advice when I really needed it."

By the 1988 North American, Attla certainly knew Kokrine was a serious dog musher, but Kokrine hadn't been a champion. He hovered near the front of the pack, but didn't seem able to put everything together to make the big push for first place. To some extent, Attla kept thinking of Kokrine as a boy who had played with his own children, and he couldn't see him for the man and racer he'd grown into. In addition, Kokrine, much like his mentor, was good at the psyche game. "George," he would say, "my dogs are just no good. They won't run." George believed him. And so George was ripe to be taken.

"Marvin is the type of racer who keeps your mind off him as much as he can," said Attla. "He's not a threat. He was always in the race, but not a winner. You pick certain people as winners, and I'd known Marvin since he was in the juniors. I never pictured Marvin as a winner. He doesn't talk. He never tells you he had a good team. The dogs are always doing horrible, according to him. But he was always right in there somewhere.

"During the North American, I never realized the kid was beating me until I was almost across the finish line. He fooled me."

Kokrine won the race by about fifteen seconds after lying in third place entering the final heat. Attla was in first place by Sunday's heat. Attla was more worried about Charlie Stevens placing second and Len Robb placing fourth than about anything Kokrine could throw at him.

"Marvin never entered my mind when we took off for the thirty-mile heat," said Attla.

Attla was traveling the trail with a portable radio, listening to the reports. Within four miles, he heard that Stevens had crashed and his dogs had lost their willingness to run, so he mentally scratched Stevens as a contender. Then he heard that Robb caught Kokrine, so it sounded like Marvin's poor-mouthing was all true, that he did have dogs who didn't want to run.

"So I'm just kind of coasting along, and it looks like I've got this race, you know?" said Attla.

He figured Robb couldn't catch him because his team would burn out from the fast start. He wondered about Charlie Champaine making a late charge. Champaine was moving fast. Hmm, thought Attla. He almost missed it when the announcer said Kokrine had repassed Robb.

All of this activity was happening behind Attla. As the overall leader, he earned the right to be the first one on the trail for that day, and anyone coming from behind had to make up the staggered start.

"I must have been about four miles from home when I heard on the radio that Marvin was faster than me at the checkpoints," said Attla, "that he could beat me. So I got everything out of my dogs the last four miles, but when I crossed the finish line, I was hearing that Marvin was faster at the checkpoints."

Attla had to stand at the finish line and watch as Kokrine chugged home a few seconds faster to claim the North American.

"He really surprised me," said George. "I thought, 'You don't have to wonder about him.' He comes over every day in the winter telling me what a bad dog team he has."

Not that year, though, that's for sure.

"George has beat me most of my life as a dog musher," said Kokrine. "But not that time. It's only been in the last couple of years I've ever beaten him. You've got to pay the price."

Chapter 27

Roots

It is spring in Galena, the sun is high in the sky, the hours of daylight are long. The snow remains piled high by the homes in the Yukon River community of about six hundred people, but it is softening, melting gradually.

There is a different texture to the air in springtime in the Alaska Bush. The wind out of the north is gentler. It doesn't carry the same sting, the same bite as it does in fall. This wind heralds not the soon-arriving bitterness of winter, but the soon-arriving warmth of summer. One is a slap, the other a kiss.

It is a time of optimism, of celebration, and the traditional spring carnival at the end of March is an invitation to the people to let loose and party. They have been cooped up all winter in their cabins, fighting the elements. Now they can play outdoors without fear of frostbite, without the gloom of long night.

All across the Interior, in the tiny villages along the Yukon and Koyukuk Rivers, it is the season of release. The carnivals come in a series. First it's Galena's turn. Then Nulato's and Tanana's. Huslia, Hughes, and Allakaket, much smaller places, take turns hosting a carnival in rotating years.

The people come from miles around the community, often traveling by snowmachine. There are games of skill and reunions among families, snowshoe races, and dances in the evening. The cornerstone of the carnival, though, is the dog race, just as it was when George Attla was growing up.

Attla, twenty years removed from living in the village, has never forgotten the pleasures of spring carnival, and despite the passage of years as he has become more and more of a famous figure throughout the state, he regularly returns to his roots in the spring.

When he goes home to the villages, Attla goes as a conquering hero. Everyone knows the Huslia Hustler. It is an event when George comes to town. There is a relative and old friend in most every town. Although the races carry big purses—as much as ten thousand dollars—the atmosphere is less intense than it is in the big cities of Anchorage and Fairbanks.

On the visits to Galena, Attla stays with his brother Robert, whose home turns into Mushing Central. In the days leading up to the two-day race, all the mushers in town, perhaps ten or a dozen, crowd into Robert's kitchen. They sit around the table, and George holds court, telling stories. Or the mushers ask for advice.

"All the local mushers want to talk to him," said Robert. "They can learn from him. Our house gets to be a pretty busy place when he comes. Everyone roots for George all year in the other races, and they cheer for him when he comes to Galena. But he's also the visiting team. There is always a local favorite who would like to beat George Attla."

The village racing scene is an underpublicized world. The events dominate local conversation, but people in Anchorage or Fairbanks don't even realize they are taking place. The focus of the sprint mushing season is the Fur Rendezvous and the North American for them. By the time the village races start, far from the media centers, far removed from the population centers, streets are bare in Southcentral Alaska. Most of the snow is gone. People in Anchorage are turning their thoughts to summer activities. They're preparing for the fishing season, for bicycle riding, and for other pursuits. Another dog race with perhaps a dozen entries is of only passing interest.

For Attla, though, the annual spring trip north is invigorating. He enjoys the visits now more than ever, since it is a revisitation to his youth, and his status built over the years makes his arrival and participation something special for the communities. "The feelings out there haven't changed over the years," said Attla. "You're welcome, and the people treat you well. They all know me. And I go home and see all my old friends and the guys I grew up with. It's a homecoming. The feeling is really something that's hard to describe. They make me feel special. Even in the villages where I don't have relatives, I stay in the homes of people I've known all my life. It's a family feeling there, too. It's almost like turning back the clock. It hasn't changed."

George Attla coming to town is as significant to Huslia or Hughes as a visit from Ronald Reagan would be to Tampico, Illinois.

"Everybody is so happy to see him," said Rose Ambrose of Attla's stops in Huslia. "The families, all the relatives are there. It's a real happy time. All of the young people know who he is, even if they're never met him. He meets all of the kids of the people he's known."

One of Attla's greatest spring mushing adventures occurred in 1991.

Usually, the biggest obstacle to any visit Attla pays to the villages is the cost of travel. Flying within the state of Alaska often seems disproportionately expensive compared to flights to destinations out of state. That cost is greatly compounded if you are attempting to transport a team of up to sixteen dogs in comfort. There have been times when Attla has cancelled spring racing plans only because he couldn't afford to take his dogs on the road. He figured out that even if he won the races, he would lose money, so he stayed home.

In the spring of 1991, Attla came up with a better idea. He and a friend, Jim Orrison, and Orrison's wife, Elaine, decided to hook up sleds to snowmachines and blaze trail. They started in Manley, about a hundred and fifty miles north of North Pole on the highway, and drove the machines the remaining several hundred miles north to the villages. They packed up their survival gear and boxes for thirty-one dogs, then set off on a three-week trip, hopping from community to community in a three-snowmachine caravan.

"If you have to fly out to the villages—and to get to some of them you have to hire a charter—it's expensive," said Attla. "You have to win two of the races just to break even, and you'd have to win three races to come out a little bit ahead. So Jim and I planned all winter to haul the dogs out there. Nobody had done it before. We built toboggans like a regular dog box behind a truck. It was a lot of fun."

This experimental journey got off to a slow start. It took Attla and his crew about three hours to go the first fifteen miles out of Manley. At that rate, they wouldn't make the villages until the following autumn. They hadn't packed properly, and they were just creeping along. The gear was piled high, as if they were prospectors coming into the country in pursuit of gold.

"We were expecting to go fast," said Attla. "But we couldn't get up the hills."

At that point, Attla was wondering if flying wasn't the way to go after all. After all the planning, they weren't getting anywhere. They readjusted the loads, repacked, and tied the three snowmachines together with the lead snowmachine empty. That worked, and they buzzed across the land, picking up speed.

The Attla and Orrison express explored the country and pulled into villages, making stops like a train crossing the west. The weather was nice, and it was like being on tour.

The first stop was Galena, and Attla, who had raced poorly that winter, had another disaster. The event was so depressing, he thought it might have been a message that he should have stayed home.

Only a few miles into the race, the trail was obscured. All the teams took a wrong turn and had to double back. Attla was one of those who misjudged the trail, but as he was turning his team, the tow lines became tangled. The rope wrapped itself around one dog's neck, and the dog strangled in harness. These type of fluke accidents occur periodically. Mushers can't predict such bad luck, and they are usually powerless to do anything.

Despite dampened spirits, Attla and Orrison continued to Nulato, perhaps a hundred miles west through the Innoko National Wildlife Refuge and along the Yukon River.

In Nulato, Attla's luck improved. Competing against a group of local racers, he won the two-day race of sixteen-mile heats. It was his first victory of the season.

Attla took note of some of the high quality of racing dogs, and it reminded him of the way life was in the Fifties, when village mushers pooled their dogs to form a hot team capable of racing against the best in the world.

"I think that could happen again," said Attla. "I think they could get a competitive team up that way. It's not happening now, but it could. There are a lot of good dog people out there in the villages still. Not as many as there used to be when my father and Sidney Huntington had dogs, because the younger generation wasn't raised with dogs like we were. But there are some people. It's a world we don't know much about now. There might be a great musher who just needs a chance. There might be another George Attla out there."

A week after winning in Nulato, Attla and Orrison chugged on to Hughes. Shannon Erhart was driving the Curtis Erhart team there, and Chuck Erhart was entered, too. Earlier in the season, during the Rendezvous, Sue, one of Attla's leaders, injured a wrist. But now Sue was healed. She gave George's team a boost, and Attla beat both of the Erhart brothers' teams to take the title in Hughes.

Attla had two straight wins, and Orrison, running a team of Attla yearlings, raced well, too, with a third place in Galena. And those were dogs just racing for experience. The villages were still being very good to George Attla. "We had a really good time," said Attla. "I was glad I did it, and I'll do it again."

In 1992, Attla did try a similar plan. He found that hauling dogs by snowmachine worked, and it was so much cheaper than flying. That spring, he finished off his winter campaign with winning appearances in Tanana and Allakaket.

"It went really well," he said. "It was a good way to end the season."

Chapter 28

Mellowing

As the decade of the Eighties turned to the Nineties, George Attla was still in contention for top honors in every race he entered.

The season of 1989 belonged to Roxy Wright-Champaine, though. She won everything. And Attla finished second in everything, in preliminary races, in the Rendezvous, and in the North American. There was no reason to think that Attla would drop into a racing slump. The Champaines' dominance would run its course, and then Attla would start winning again. But such a turnaround was slow to come.

From second in the 1989 Rondy, Attla dropped to fourth in the 1990 race. He was sixth in 1991, when he had to carry home an unprecedented four dogs in the sled basket. Then he was fifth in 1992. His was no longer the first name mentioned among the challengers to the Champaine dynasty.

Things were even worse in the North American. Attla placed a sad fourteenth in 1991 and sixth in 1992.

In the 1991 North American, Attla was cruising along in about fifth place, seventeen miles into the first heat when his team got tangled with another musher's.

"My dogs got in a big muddle," said Attla. "I got the dogs loose from his team, but I had knots in my team. When they strung out there was a half-hitch in the tow line. The rope went around a dog's neck, and it strangled. I was last that day. I finished way off the pace. I killed one dog, which I had never done, ever, in my career. I finished last in the North American, and I had never run last."

It was only a few weeks later in Galena that another dog died in harness.

Two dogs in only a month. Things seemed to be falling apart. What was going on? Why was Attla falling behind.?

For one thing, the quality of competition was better than ever. Once upon a time, perhaps Attla had only to worry about the skills of Roland Lombard and Gareth Wright as the only mushers of his caliber. Now newcomers were popping up, and they had fast dogs and desire, too.

"In the late Sixties and Seventies, it was just Doc Lombard and me," said Attla. "But starting in the Eighties, there were a whole bunch of guys on my heels who could beat me. I think there are more good dogs than ever. Everybody has a good team. Before, the dogs were concentrated in just a few people's hands. Now they're scattered all over. There's not just one threat anymore.

"There are more people interested in dog mushing, more people doing it, and they're getting really good at it. They've put their time in. They were in the small races, they got experience, and they got better. It used to be something a musher would do on the side. Now you've got all kinds of experts racing dogs, veterinarians, doctors, scientists who study everything."

The state of the art was a far cry from going on instinct, from picking up a dog to guess its weight, from getting a sense of the dog simply by gazing at it. It was, it might be said, like comparing modem medicine to homespun remedies.

"When I started, you had to develop the experience by trial and error," said Attla. "You had to do everything. Now, you can pick up a book and read how to win, how to feed them, how to train them, the whole thing. Even how to ride a sled. It's really changing."

Marvin Kokrine, who had a couple of near-misses in the North American in the early Nineties, said there's more stacked against Attla now than ever before. "He's still trying to be the best," said Kokrine, "and it might still be in him. He's got the track record, but he's got to overcome more now than he did. There's a lot of young dog mushers in their prime. That makes it harder to find good dogs."

The days are long gone, said Kokrine, when a musher in the village could make the sport a seasonal occupation with only a handful of working dogs. Now, sprint dog mushing is a year-round proposition in terms of planning, breeding, and training.

"Life isn't the same as it was," he said. "When George started, there was no such things as snow-gos. The dogs were raised as part of the family. They never had an easy life."

Kokrine said it costs him three to four thousand dollars a month to maintain a kennel "just to keep racing."

And not only that, but top-notch dogs are scarce. Either you breed them or you don't find them, he said. The growth of the Iditarod has made a big difference. Whereas once the only mushing was over shorter distances, now a large core of mushers breed dogs only for long distances. Some focus only on middle distances, and of course, some concentrate only on sprinting.

"People are getting specialized," said Kokrine. "This is a lifestyle and a very expensive lifestyle."

For the most part, Attla has kept up with the changing times and over the years has been an innovator. He stayed one step ahead of the other mushers for decades, building his unmatched record.

"It's easy to forget that, with the popularity of the Iditarod, and with Susan Butcher and Rick Swenson winning regularly, it's a lot easier to dominate long distance mushing, because it has a shorter history," said Jim Welch. "It's easier to perpetuate a line of trotting dogs that are good at that middle distance kind of speed than it is to have quality sprint dogs."

One major problem Attla has faced in recent years is a lack of first-rate leaders. No dog like Freckles or Trot has emerged from his kennel. He has dogs with speed, but no dogs with the kind of common sense the boss is looking for. Moses and Grace did a good job in the North American in the late Eighties, but by 1990, they were too old, and there were no first-class replacements handy.

"That's been my weakness," said Attla, "the leaders. It really showed up. I was weak in front. I think the team I ran in 1991 was one of the best dog teams I ever had, but there was just nobody to run in front, and things went wrong all year. It was a horrible year, the worst year racing I ever had. There were just constant problems."

The tone for the racing campaign was set in Attla's first race of the season in December 1990, at Montana Creek, a race about a hundred miles from Anchorage. Within the first five minutes of the first heat, his dogs were passing another team and got tangled up with the other dogs. No leadership.

It might be said that Attla's team never did get untangled that year.

"It started horribly, right from the start," he said. "I couldn't get by that dog team. I was just tied up in knots. I had to unsnap my dogs completely from the sled to get them untangled. I had seven dogs running around loose. That was the first time ever in racing I had to do that."

Soon after, at the Orville Lake Memorial in Anchorage, Attla thought he had found his leaders. Sue and Lobo emerged and did well. But the feeling of optimism was quickly lost at the Alaska Mill and Feed Race in Anchorage and at another race in Big Lake, fifty miles north of Anchorage. The leaders just wouldn't lead. They were easily distracted, didn't respond to commands, and as a result, the team didn't do the job. "I thought they were good enough to win," said Attla. "But nobody would run in front of them. It was frustrating. I couldn't get a good run out of them."

It's quite possible, too, that the leader standing on the back of the sled that season wasn't doing his share of leading, either. "I wasn't as intense as I should have been," said Attla. "I think I was missing something."

Alfred, one of George's younger brothers, teased him rather harshly, offering a wakeup call of sorts akin to Eddy Streeper's. "I think you're getting too mellow," Alfred told George. "You're too mellow for a champion. I don't think you can be a champion now. I just think you're too easygoing. You're not chewing nails."

Instead of getting angry, as he might have, Attla grew reflective and found himself agreeing with Alfred to some extent. "I got to thinking maybe he was right," said Attla. "During the summer, after the racing season, I try to figure things out, what I did wrong, why I'm running this badly. That goes through my mind a lot. He may be right in a way."

There is conflicting evidence, though. Old friend Bill Sturdevant has argued mushing philosophy with Attla regularly over the years. The two men are close friends, but they don't mitigate opinions. They express them bluntly.

"He still wants to argue with me continuously," said Sturdevant. "We have rip-roaring arguments. One time in the late Seventies, when there was a tendency to take a drink after a race, we had a fistfight in the house and it spilled over to outside. Lifelong friends have got to be allowed to express their feelings. Being competitors as well as friends, there can be a lot of tension."

Clearly, the man had the fire. Does Attla still have that kind of passion? Maybe so.

After the first day of the 1992 Fur Rendezvous, Attla asked Sturdevant to drive the sixty miles from his home in Knik into Anchorage to study the dog teams and give him his analysis. As usual, Sturdevant was forthright, and he told Attla he didn't think he had all his dogs in the team set up in the proper order.

"And then I listened to him rant and rave at me," said Sturdevant. That could mean Attla is only sort of semi-relaxed.

Attla said he thinks his father, George, Sr., mellowed considerably in his later years, and he may just be following in his path.

"When we were young and he said something, you listened," said Attla. "You did whatever he told you. When he was getting older, he mellowed out. I remember when I was a kid, he used to tell my mother, 'We'll do this, we'll do that,' and my mother would say, 'Whatever you say is fine.' But when he got older, I know my mom was telling him what to do. I used to tease him about it and say, 'Hey, what's wrong with you? She's the boss. She's telling you what to do.'"

Could it really be true that as he approaches sixty years of age, George Attla is getting soft? "It could very well be," he said laughing. "Maybe I'm enjoying myself too much with my kids. That could be it."

No other musher, however, has suggested Attla is over the hill lately. Not within his earshot, anyway.

"Maybe there are people thinking that," said Attla, "that, 'He should have quit when he was on top.' But don't count me out yet. I haven't quit yet. I don't have the leaders. If I get the dogs to run up front, then we'll see what happens."

What happens, Attla hopes, is another world championship.

Chapter 29

Elusive Edge

When he won his tenth world championship in 1982, George Attla never would have imagined it would be the last world title listed on his resume. Never.

Attla could never again recapture the magic that catapulted him to the zenith of the sport. The ageless musher soldiered on, breeding new litters of puppies, mixing and matching leaders, experimenting with fresh combinations, but he could never again find the right mix of dogs to bring him to the top of the heap.

As Attla approached sixty his hunger for victory remained strong. One more title was his refrain. He was convinced he could do it, convinced that one final championship would be the crowning glory of his astonishing career.

Fellow competitors would not hazard the guess that it was too late for him, that it was time for younger mushers to take over and permanently push Attla to the side. Attla retained too much respect — and, of course, there was always the real chance he would prove doubters wrong.

During the 1980s and into the early 1990s, one way Attla sought to make up for his shortcoming in savvy leaders was to invest heavily in buying other breeders' dogs.

"I buy a lot of dogs," said Attla a decade after his final championship run. "An amazing number of dogs. Every spring when I get beat, I look around the yard and say, 'I've got to buy X number of dogs to overcome how I lost this year.' I have the dogs picked out that I've seen that I want and I go out and try to get them. It's been that way for a quite a few years. By the beginning of the fall, the team that's supposed to be the championship team, in my mind, is sitting in the yard."

For Attla, fall was like spring training for a baseball manager, evaluating and assembling talent for the campaign ahead.

Although he did not win major titles, Attla remained in the mix, always placing high in the key events of the season. The tantalizing near-misses were even more frustrating for him. It kept him hoping that one more great win was within reach. All this time, others in the mushing community dicussed the topic of, Can George do it? Opinion vacillated.

Former champion Gareth Wright suggested that Attla had to win again by the time he turned sixty because his body wouldn't be able to withstand the rigors of three days of hard racing any longer. Friend Jim Welch felt it was more a mindset issue with Attla—did he retain the necessary killer instinct?

Steven Attla, George's brother, found it incredible that the ten-time champion was still racing at all as he entered his seventh decade.

"He's only got one good leg and only got one good eye," said Steven, "and he still keeps going. It's really something when you think about it. I always think he should quit, but he's still in there with the leaders. He wants one more championship and he'll do it if he ever gets the chance."

But year after year passed. Season after season came and went without another Attla world title. Gradually, he began to wonder if there wasn't something wrong with the musher. Perhaps the human member of the team had grown too complacent?

"Maybe I've lost the edge somewhere in there," said Attla after ten years of going home to North Pole empty-handed from the Fur Rendezvous. "Maybe I just enjoy it too much. I think that in order to be the best, there has to be a little misery associated with it somewhere. Maybe my dogs have figured me out. I always raised dogs to suit my personality. Maybe my dogs aren't tough enough anymore because I'm not tough enough."

In the early 1990s, in his quest to regain his place in sprint mushing, Attla did something he'd never tried before. He heard that Rudy Summers in Huslia had a knack for training leaders. He wondered if Rudy had the hard edge Attla felt was missing in himself. So he sent two two-year-old dogs to Summers for training.

"I've never had other people train a leader for me before," said Attla, "but he might be able to teach them something that I can't. It's very possible technology has passed me by. As far as training dogs, and racing them, I know those things. But the feeding and care of animals — like how many hours before a race you should feed them — I'm not as good as I should be and I never have been. So those things could be in the way. People are always coming up with new ways or better ways to feed dogs."

The dogged pursuit of an eleventh world championship kept Attla tinkering and planning and training. He even mused aloud that once he accomplished the feat he wouldn't retire, but laughingly he said he'd return to the 1,100-mile Iditarod and try that again.

But there was no next title. No last glory ride. In 1994, Attla placed seventh in the Fur Rendezvous. In 1995, he scratched. He was a "DNF," did not finish. Thirty-seven years after his splashy debut in Anchorage, it was last appearance in the race that made him famous. His body simply could not cope with the rigors of hard racing on back-to-back-to-back days anymore.

After ten Fur Rondy world titles and eight North American victories, Attla was through with championship-caliber, three-day racing.

"I don't have the strength," said Attla. "Physically, I don't think I can do it."

Chapter 30

The Greatest

These days the old musher is a homebody.

And a coach. For Frankie and Shay. His youngest children made their racing debuts in Fairbanks during the winter of 1999-2000. On one day, Frankie won the four-dog class and Shay won the two-dog class.

"You know what I'm really proud of," said the gray-haired George Attla, including all eight of his children in the thought. "My kids turned out well."

The North Pole dog yard may not be as crowded as it once was, but entering the winter of 2000-2001. Attla had twenty grown dogs, eleven puppies, and two litters on the way. Gradually, he is rebuilding the excellence into his team.

"I'm thinking I'm gonna have a dog team by the time Frankie turns eighteen," said Attla, cackling with the same confident laugh he used to display when he was in prime as a racer.

Although Attla backed off from entering the major championship races in the mid-1990s, he did not retire from mushing altogether. He continued to contest shorter races in the outlying villages where his name is revered. He regularly returned to the spring carnival circuit in the communities of the Koyukuk River.

Then in the spring of 1999, Attla went home to Huslia, the place that spawned him and bestowed his nickname "The Huslia

Hustler" so long ago. Standing behind fourteen dogs on the sled runners, Attla won the first-day heat. But it snowed overnight and the fresh snow conditions made the going tougher. An aching Attla slowed and placed third overall.

"The old man couldn't do nothing in the snow," he joked.

Appropriately enough, come full circle, that was Attla's last race. He announced his retirement, ending his active career as a musher in the sport he loved and made his living at for more than forty years. Attla overcame illnesses and injuries, but although he held it off longer than most, he couldn't overcome the advancement of time.

A dominant figure on the Alaskan sports scene for the better part of a half century, Attla's profile had receded after he began passing up the major sprint events. But the arrival of the 21st century helped rekindle awareness and awe for Attla's career achievements.

On January 1, 2000, the *Anchorage Daily News* announced a list of its top 100 Alaskan athletes of the century and Attla was ranked No. 2.

Similarly, the *Fairbanks Daily News-Miner* selected Attla as the greatest musher of all time.

Attla was gone from the scene, but not forgotten. He reveled in the new attention. People walked up to him on the street, congratulating him. They lauded him anew for his record-setting era.

"It was just a renewing of respect from people," said Attla.

In all, the fresh praise was basically fresh validation, putting to paper what many around Alaska viewed as foregone fact — that Attla is mushing's greatest performer.

"I think history shows that George is the best that's ever been," said old rival Charlie Champaine.

Old friend Bill Sturdevant had the most creative idea for honoring Attla.

"What we need to do is create a State Legend," said Sturdevant. "He would be the first."

Attla does not choose to boast "I am the greatest" in Muhammad Ali style. But he is pleased when others say it. He glowed after the Alaska State Legislature passed a resolution in 1998 commending him for his decades in the sport and accomplishments. The resolution, in part, cited Attla for being an inspiration to others.

"There is extra satisfaction for me when they say I've inspired someone," said Attla, reflecting on the honor, "with the handicaps I had, that I was able to overcome. There's a satisfaction in proving that things could be done. I hope that other people who have problems would look at me and say, 'If he could do that, I can do that.' I could say anything I wanted, but it doesn't mean as much until someone else says it. To have the whole state say it, that's something."

Attla said he finally decided to retire when he realized his body wouldn't permit him to realistically compete for first place.

"I've always gone into the race with the idea of winning," he said.

One thing that eased the transition to retirement was Attla's record. His longevity is unassailable, and there is no one active within hailing distance of his victory totals in major championships, either. A combined eighteen Rondy and North American golds is a record that is sure to stand for a while — perhaps for eternity.

"I'm really proud of it," said Attla. "Nobody will ever get that many wins. It's not going to be broken. Not in my time."

Helping his youngsters learn the sport has proven immensely enjoyable. Attla was surprised how much fun he had tutoring Frankie and Shaylin through their first winter of racing.

"They were so excited about what they were doing," said Attla. "As you get older you live through somebody else's accomplishments."

In the preceding year, Attla, the father of eight and grandfather of ten, became a great-grandfather of two, raising the question of whether there will be others coming along who can use his help to master mushing.

After all, they would be learning from the best.

About the Author

Lew Freedman is a popular author of books about Alaska as well as award-winning columnist and sports editor for the *Anchorage Daily News*.

Freedman's numerous books about the northern state and its people include three books about the Iditarod Trail Sled Dog Race. His bestseller is *Iditarod Classics: Tales of the Trail from the Men and Women Who Race Across Alaska.*

A graduate of Boston University, Freedman has a master's degree from Alaska Pacific University. He and his wife, Donna, have a daughter, Abby.

More Mushing Books from Epicenter Press

JON VAN ZYLE'S IDITAROD MEMORIES

Illustrations by Jon Van Zyle • Stories by Jona Van Zyle
#887 - Hardbound - $16.95
This handsome gift book contains colorful
reproductions of the annual Iditarod posters and
stories to go with them.

HONEST DOGS

Brian Patrick O'Donoghue
#778 - Softbound - $16.95
Enjoy the drama of the race through this punishing
personal journey.

IDITAROD COUNTRY

Tricia Brown
Photos by Jeff Shultz
#666 - Hardbound - $16.95
Follow the historic trail to Native villages,
abandoned gold-mining towns, remote lodges and homesteads.

FATHER OF THE IDITAROD

Lew Freedman
#755 - Softbound - $16.95
An inspirational biography of Joe Redington, the man
who founded the thrilling 1,000-mile race.

ADVENTURES OF THE IDITAROD AIR FORCE

Ted Mattson
#593- Softbound - $12.95
Colorful, exciting stories of volunteer pilots supporting the race.

IDITAROD DREAMS

Lew Freedman & DeeDee Jonrowe
#291 - Softbound - $13.95
An absorbing account of a year in the life of a musher
preparing for the Iditarod.

**Order these and other exciting books about Alaska at
our website: www.EpicenterPress.com
Or order by phone - 800-950-6663**